Introduction to
ANALYSIS
of
VARIANCE

D0646165

Introduction to
ANALYSIS
of
VARIANCE

Design, Analysis, & Interpretation

J. Rick Turner
Julian F. Thayer

Sage Publications
International Educational and Professional Publisher
Thousand Oaks ■ London ■ New Delhi

For information:

Sage Publications, Inc.
2455 Teller Road
Thousand Oaks, California 91320
E-mail: order@sagepub.com

Sage Publications Ltd.
6 Bonhill Street
London EC2A 4PU
United Kingdom

Sage Publications India Pvt. Ltd.
M-32 Market
Greater Kailash I
New Delhi 110 048 India

Printed in the United States of America

Library of Congress Cataloging-in-Publication Data

Turner, J. Rick.
   Introduction to analysis of variance:
  Design, analysis, and interpretation /
  by J. Rick Turner and Julian F. Thayer.
     p. cm.
   Includes index.
   ISBN 0-8039-7074-9 (cloth: acid-free paper)
   ISBN 0-8039-7075-7 (pbk.:acid-free paper)
   1. Analysis of variance. I. Thayer, Julian F. II. Title.
   QA279 .T86 2001
   519.5'38—dc21   00-013065

This book is printed on acid-free paper.

03   04   05   06   7   6   5   4   3   2

Acquisition Editor:	C. Deborah Laughton
Editorial Assistant:	Eileen Carr
Production Editor:	Sanford Robinson
Editorial Assistant:	Cindy Bear
Typesetter:	Technical Typesetting, Inc.
Cover Designer:	Michelle Lee

CONTENTS

PREFACE

This book introduces you to one of the most powerful and widely used statistical techniques in experimental behavioral science research, namely, Analysis of Variance (ANOVA). Knowledge of this technique will enable you to investigate and answer a vast array of research questions. Once an experiment has been conducted, or run, the data that have been collected need to be analyzed, and so knowledge of statistics is necessary at that time. However, knowledge of statistical analysis is also necessary *before* the experiment is run. Each statistical analysis dictates that the data it analyzes must have been collected in a certain manner. In other words, when designing an experiment, we should know what analyses we intend to perform on our data to answer our research questions, and we must collect our data in the appropriate manner.

Experimental design and statistical analysis are therefore totally dependent on each other. It is impossible to separate them, and the words "design" and "analysis" are almost interchangeable in many instances. To design an experiment in the best possible way to investigate a topic of interest, we must know what analyses will best answer our questions. Then we must design our experiment in a manner that will allow those analyses to be used. And, having collected our data, we must know how to analyze them and how to *interpret* the results of our analyses. The appropriate interpretation of results of statistical analyses is absolutely crucial. The mathematical answers provided by the analyses need to be interpreted in the context of our research question. We shall come back to the issue of interpretation time and time again.

This book has two goals. First, it introduces you to different kinds of ANOVAs and explains which design/analysis is appropriate to answer certain questions. Second, it shows you how each analysis is performed and teaches you how to do these analyses using only a calculator. The second goal is important, even though you may well perform these analyses using a computer later on. Seeing how the analyses are actually done will give you a much better "feel" for the analyses than simply seeing the mathematical answers on a computer printout. While computers are very useful for conducting analyses because they can crunch enormous amounts of data in an unbelievably short time, we still need to tell computers which analyses to perform, and, once they have done so, we need to interpret the results they provide.

The first chapter explains why the statistical techniques of ANOVA are useful when designing and analyzing experimental behavioral science research. The second chapter introduces the statistical terms that are necessary to do the analyses discussed in this book. It is possible that you are already familiar with these basic terms from previous courses you may have taken. However, this chapter has been included so that any of you who have not encountered these terms before will not be at a disadvantage.

Chapters 3 through 7 introduce you to five ANOVA designs and show you exactly how they work. Chapter 8 provides some tips for tests that you may have to take and contains a summary of the five designs discussed in previous chapters. Finally, Chapter 9 shows how the "feel" for statistics that you will have acquired by working through the examples in the text can be helpful in everyday settings, such as determining how much credibility to place in claims made about products that you might be interested in purchasing.

This book deals only with one-factor and two-factor ANOVAs (a "factor" is an influence upon behavior that you wish to study). A one-factor design, for example, can be used to investigate the influence of the factor Age on memory. Two-factor designs can investigate two influences (perhaps Age and Type of Information to Be Remembered) in the same experiment, *and can investigate any interactive effects between the two factors.* You will find that one-factor and two-factor analyses are adequate for many experimental projects, but the technique can certainly be expanded to include three or more factors. By that stage, a computer becomes almost essential, because the hand calculation needed to perform the required analyses is tedious. However, if you understand the principles of one-factor and two-factor analysis of variance, you will be able to interpret the results from ANOVAs involving three or more factors.

Throughout the text, we have used various devices to emphasize specific items that will maximize your understanding of ANOVA. The first time a statistical term is introduced it is highlighted in **boldface** type. Key points and concepts are typed in *italics* (this has occurred three times already in this preface). Italic print is also used during the descriptions of some computational steps to indicate alternative approaches that produce identical answers (some of you may find it easier to follow the first explanation, while others may prefer the alternative one). Finally, "Key Concepts" appear throughout the book to highlight and summarize topics discussed nearby in the text.

This book, then, provides an introduction to one of the most useful techniques for the analysis of data in experimental behavioral science research. Conducting experimental research is a highly skilled procedure. Experiments must be designed and analyzed properly, and they must be run with meticulous care. You will be able to learn about research methodology and about other statistical techniques from other sources. However, when you have finished this book, if your appetite for research has been whetted, and you have realized that doing the necessary statistical analysis is far from impossible, then this book will have done its job.

J. Rick Turner
Julian F. Thayer

ACKNOWLEDGMENTS

First and foremost, we thank C. Deborah Laughton, our Acquiring Editor at Sage Publications, for her support throughout this project. Her advice on both content and presentation has been superb, and, quite simply, this book would not have been possible without her help. We also thank Sanford Robinson, Senior Production Editor at Sage, and Tina Burke at Technical Typesetting Incorporated.

John J. Sollers III, Ph.D., provided expert assistance with electronic manipulation of the text and the creation of the graphics used in the book, and Rachel Nabors-Oberg, M.S., double-checked all computational aspects.

One author (JFT) used draft manuscripts of this text to teach statistics classes at the Pennsylvania State University, the University of Columbia–Missouri, and the University of Bergen. Students in these classes provided invaluable feedback on the strengths and weaknesses of those initial drafts. Four anonymous reviewers also provided extremely constructive comments on the most recent draft, and the final text benefited considerably from their input.

Sincere thanks are expressed to everyone.

PART

1

INTRODUCTION

THE NEED FOR ANALYSIS
OF VARIANCE

Introduction

The study of the behavioral sciences has major differences from the study of the physical sciences. In the physical sciences, the outcome of an experiment will be exactly the same every time the experiment is performed (if it is done under the same conditions). For example, if we drop a ball from 100 feet above the ground, it will always accelerate toward the ground at a rate governed by gravity. When dealing with experiments in the behavioral sciences and the biological sciences, however, this is not the case. This book focuses on behavioral science research.

Consider this simple task, called a **reaction time task**. Your job is to watch a bulb, and as soon as it becomes lit you are to press a button with your index finger. The surroundings are quiet, and there are no distractions. The time between the **stimulus onset**, when the bulb becomes lit, and your response is recorded in hundredths of a second. This time is a measure of your **reaction time**. You may be surprised to learn that if you are asked to do this 10 times, that is, if you perform 10 **trials**, it is entirely possible that you will record five, six, or even more different reaction times. This is true despite the fact that you were trying just as hard to be as fast as possible on all trials.

These differences in a person's reaction times are the result of innate variation in the nervous system. Because of this variation, the individual's perceptual, central processing, and motor response systems will respond slightly differently each time he or she is given exactly the same reaction time task. Similarly, people will respond slightly differently on different trials in many different kinds of experiments. This is one source of variation in data we collect during behavioral science research.

On top of these differences, all humans are different from each other, thus introducing another source of variation to behavioral science research. Going back to the example of the reaction time task, Person A may always respond relatively quickly, even though individual response times vary from trial to trial, while Person B may always respond relatively slowly.

Dealing with both kinds of variation, that is, *finding meaningful answers to our research questions despite this variation*, is the goal of our statistical analyses.

A Research Question and an Experiment Designed to Answer It

A brand new make of racing car has just been built. The final piece of instrumentation is a warning system that will warn the driver of a particular problem. The question is: Should the driver be warned by a visual signal or by an auditory signal? That is, will the driver react more quickly to a light or to a sound? One simple way to find the answer, it may seem, is to set up a reaction time task in a laboratory and get a **subject** or **participant** (see next section), probably a racing car driver, to take part in this experiment. Give the subject the two signals, one at a time, and see which leads to the smaller (i.e., quicker) reaction time.

However, things are not as simple as they first appeared. The first problem we have to deal with is **order effects**. That is, will the subject react quicker to the first signal or to the second signal, *despite* which signal is actually given when? The second problem is that, as we have just noted, one test of any given subject's reaction to a stimulus is not a good, representative estimate of the reaction time that most accurately characterizes that person's performance. The third problem is, who should we choose to be the subject? We want the answer we get to be **generalizable** to all drivers, not just to the one driver whom we choose for the experiment. As we noted earlier, everyone is different from each other. So, testing only one driver is unlikely to lead to a generalizable finding.

So, how about we test, say, 20 drivers for their responses to both stimuli, and each person does each test 10 times, that is, has 10 **trials** per stimulus? The trials are also presented in **counterbalanced order**. That is, half of the drivers, chosen at random, receive the light stimulus trials first, while the other half receive the sound stimulus first. (This is a simple counterbalancing strategy; much more complex ones can be devised depending on the nature of a given experiment. However, the goal of all such strategies, namely, dealing with potential order effects, is the same.)

Our experiment is now taking shape. Once we have all of those numbers (all 400 of them), we need statistical analyses to help us reach our decision. Because individuals differ in their responses to exactly the same task on different trials, and because we are using 20 different drivers in this experiment, we know that there is bound to be variation in our data. What statistics will help us to decide is whether there is **systematic variation** in our data. That is, do the responses to one stimulus tend to be higher (or lower) than the responses to the other, despite the fact that one person may be fairly slow on both occasions and another person relatively fast on both occasions?

This is one way of expressing the basic question a statistical analysis will help us answer: Are these two (or more) groups of numbers varying in a systematic manner? Put another way, statistics enables us to answer the question: *Are two (or more) groups of numbers sufficiently different for us to believe that they are the result of a particular influence that was operating?*

The Terms Subject and Participant

Throughout this text, we use the term *subject* to refer to a person taking part in an experiment. Some authors use the term *participant* in exactly the same way. Certain professional organizations have guidelines concerning the preferred (or mandatory) use of one term. Therefore, your instructor may recommend one or the other to you.

Getting a "Feel" for Comparing Groups of Numbers

Now that we've seen the basic philosophy behind statistical analyses, let's look at some of the important components used to do them. When we collect data in our experiments, the numbers we collect are often called **scores**. For a given set of scores, there are two useful sets of characteristics that can be used to describe them. One set describes their **central tendency**, providing a measure of their central value. The **arithmetic mean**, often called simply the **mean** (the sum of the scores divided by the total number of scores), is frequently used here. The second set describes how spread out around the central value the scores are. One measure of this spread is the **range**. The range is the arithmetic difference between the largest and the smallest value in a group of scores.

Consider these two groups of scores, A and B:

(A)   47   56   44   53   50
(B)   54   60   66   63   57

Now consider another two groups of scores, C and D:

(C)   100   70   10   20   50
(D)   10   90   60   95   45

These pairs of groups are shown in Figure 1.1.

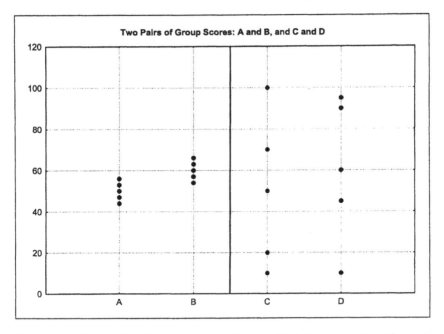

Figure 1.1. Two pairs of group scores: Do you think the groups in either pair look different from each other?

The two-part question here is: Do you think that Group A is really different from Group B, and do you think that Group C is really different from Group D? First, let's look at A and B. The means of A and B are 50 and 60, respectively. So, there is a difference between the means, a difference of 10. Now let's look at the range of each group. The range of A is 12 (56 − 44), and the range for B, coincidentally, is also 12 (66 − 54).

Second, let's look at C and D. The means of C and D are also 50 and 60, respectively, which shows that, once again, there is a difference of 10 between the means of the two groups we are comparing. Now let's look at the range of each group. The range of C is 90 (100 − 10), and the range of D is 85 (95 − 10). In comparison to the ranges of A and B, these ranges are much larger.

Now, using only these two very simple statistical measures (the mean and the range) as guidelines, do you think that Group A is really different from Group B, and do you think that Group C is really different from Group D? Well, simply looking at Figure 1.1 can probably help you to answer this two-part question. You might agree that Group A seems different from Group B, while Group C and Group D do not really seem that different.

The point of this example is that you may get these feelings *even though the difference between the means of A and B (i.e., 10) is the same as the difference between the means of C and D*. The consideration that may have been the determining factor for you is that, despite the difference in group means being identical, the *difference in ranges was considerable*.

"Key Three" Components of Statistical Analysis

College athletics has various catchphrases for conferences and events, such as the "Big 12" and the "Final Four." Using a similar catchphrase, we can think of statistical analysis as having three key components. When determining whether two (or more) groups of scores are different from each other, the "key three" components of our analysis are:

1. Variation *between* the groups (between-groups variation)

2. Variation *within* the groups (within-groups variation)

3. The total number of scores in all the groups

KEY CONCEPTS

The "Key Three" Components of Statistical Analysis

Between-Groups Variance
Within-Groups Variance
Total Number of Scores in All of the Groups

Let's consider each of these key components in turn. To determine the variation between the groups, we compare the group means. The other two components being equal, *the larger the difference between the means of two groups, the more likely we are to believe that the two groups really differ from each other.* The second component focuses on within-groups variation. The other two components being equal, *the less variation there is within groups, the more likely we are to believe that the two groups really differ from each other.* The third component focuses on how many pieces of information (data points or scores) we can use to make our decision. The other two components being equal, *the more scores we can use in our analysis, the more likely we are to believe that a given difference in group means is a real difference.*

Between- and Within-Groups Variation

The variation between the groups represents systematic variation due to the **effect** that we are interested in (type of warning signal in a racing car, or anything else that we are investigating). The variation within the groups represents variation due to **chance**, that is, random variation that is *not* due to the effect that we are investigating. Where does this variation due to chance come from? We noted earlier that humans have innate neural variation and that all humans are different from each other. These sources of variation are not directly related to the effect under investigation.

The between-groups variation and the within-groups variation for any groups of scores can be mathematically determined. When we start to do formal statistical analyses, the word *variation* will be replaced by the term **variance**. The term variance measures variation, and so the concept of the two words is the same (although variance has a precise definition and a precisely calculated value for any group of numbers). For the rest of this chapter, we'll use the term variance.

The between-groups variance is often called the **effect variance**, and the within-groups variance is often called the **error variance** (the error variance is due to chance). If the effect variance is large compared to the error variance, the groups are more likely to be defined as differing reliably. If the effect variance is small relative to the error variance, this is not so.

A good way to compare any two quantities is to form a ratio. Consider this ratio:

$$\frac{\text{Effect Variance (Between-Groups Variance)}}{\text{Error Variance (Within-Groups Variance)}}.$$

There are three possibilities of interest once this ratio has been calculated. If the effect variance is larger than the error variance, this ratio will produce a value that is larger than 1.0. If the effect variance turns out to be exactly the same as the error variance (an extremely unlikely occurrence in real life), the ratio will produce a value exactly equal to 1.0. And, if the effect variance is smaller than the error variance, this ratio will produce a value that is less than 1.0. The important point to note is this: The larger the value produced by this ratio, the more likely groups are to be truly different, and therefore to be defined by statistical analysis as different.

Total Number of Scores in All the Groups

Now let's look at the third of our "key three" components, that is, the number of scores in the groups. This consideration is quite simple: *The other components being equal, the greater the number of scores the better.* The number of scores is a measure of the **size of the study**.

Recall the example of the reaction time task. Suppose we want to obtain the reaction time of a driver to the auditory signal. If the driver did two trials, we could calculate an average. If the driver did it 10 times, we would get a better idea of that person's typical time. One hundred trials would be even better. Of course, practical considerations (the time taken to run experiments) come into play here. However, it is true that the more pieces of information we have, the better able we are to make a reliable assessment.

Consider it this way. Suppose a person's average (mean) reaction time for light was 0.36 seconds and for sound was 0.30 seconds. The difference is 0.06 seconds, i.e., six hundredths of a second. Just how much faith we put in this finding as an accurate representation depends on the number of trials performed, that is, the number of pieces of information that contributed to each mean. If the driver did each task twice, we wouldn't put much faith in the results. If there were 20 trials per stimulus, we would be much more inclined to believe the data. And, if there were 100 trials per stimulus, we would be pretty convinced. (From our discussions earlier, we would also have to know the within-groups variance before making any definitive decision.)

The amount of "faith" we put in our results can be calculated mathematically, and the number of items of information (data, or scores) we have available to analyze is one of the "key three" factors in calculating this. That is, the size of the study is an important factor in statistical analysis.

Levels of Significance

Statistical analyses tell us *how likely it is that a given (observed) result could have occurred by chance alone*. Imagine two sets of scores, A and B. The mean of A is a bit higher than the mean of B. Because the means are only a bit different, it is possible that the result could be due to chance alone. That is, although the means are indeed different, the difference between the groups may not be **reliable**. If we did the experiment again, the result could be different; this time, B might have the higher mean, or the mean of both groups may be identical. If, however, the means of A and B are sufficiently different, it is unlikely that such a difference could have arisen by chance alone. The question is: *How do we determine if an observed difference is "sufficiently" different?*

In any given case, statistical analysis will answer this question. In statistical terms, our analysis will tell us whether the groups differ **significantly** or not. That is, it will tell us whether the **effect size**, the difference between the group means, is significant. In statistics, the word *significant* has a precise meaning, and confusion with the everyday use of the word should be avoided. If a result is **statistically significant**, it tells us that the group means are too different to have been that way by chance alone. In other words, the effect under investigation had a **significant** influence.

Two **levels of significance,** $p < 0.05$ and $p < 0.01$, are typically employed in statistics. (There are others as well, but we will focus on these two.) If a particular result is judged likely to occur *less than 5 times out of* 100 *by chance alone,* this result is said to be significant at the $p < 0.05$ **level of significance.** This means that the probability of getting that result by chance alone was less than 5%. If a result is judged by our statistical analysis likely to occur *less than once in* 100 *times by chance alone,* this result is said to be significant at the $p < 0.01$ **level of significance.** The former gives us pretty good confidence that the result obtained was a true reflection of an actual difference; the latter gives us very good confidence.

We'll see how these levels are used in analyses of variance (ANOVAs) in Chapters 3 through 7. For now, we'll make this note about how we check whether our results attain statistical significance or not: For any statistic that is calculated to compare different groups, sets of **tables of critical values** exist. These tell us the magnitude that the statistic needs to attain to achieve statistical significance. Typically, there are two tables of critical values, one for the 5% level and one for the 1% level. When checking to see whether our results attain statistical significance or not, *we always start with the 5% table.* If the statistic does not reach significance in this table, *it is not possible that it will reach significance at the higher, that is, more significant, 1% level.* If the statistic does reach significance at the 5% level, we can then proceed to check whether it also does so at the 1% level.

KEY CONCEPTS

Levels of Significance

We'll focus on two important levels of significance:
$p < 0.05$, the 5% level of significance
$p < 0.01$, the 1% level of significance

Experimental Design and Statistical Analysis

Following this brief introduction to statistical analysis, we need to make an extremely important point. To use a particular analysis to examine (analyze) the results of an experiment, those results (scores) must have been collected in a specific way, which, in turn, means that the experiment must have been **designed** in a specific way. Therefore, there is a very close relationship between **experimental design** and statistical analysis, so close that the words *design* and *analysis* are almost interchangeable in this context. Each statistical analysis corresponds to a particular experimental design, and each experimental design allows the results to be analyzed by a specific statistical analysis.

Actually, the last part of the previous sentence should more accurately say "and each *good* experimental design allows the results to be analyzed by a specific statistical analysis." Some bad designs simply do not allow the results from the experiment to be analyzed in a meaningful way. Unfortunately, there are cases where large experiments have been conducted by people not familiar with statistical analysis and, therefore, not aware of the crucial relationship between design and analysis. Once the data collection is complete, these individuals have found that their results cannot be meaningfully analyzed.

Figure 1.2 captures this intimate relationship between experimental design and statistical analysis.

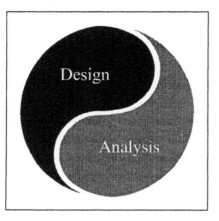

Figure 1.2. Intimate relationship between experimental design and statistical analysis.

Experimental Methodology

In addition to experimental design and statistical analysis, a third component of **running,** or conducting, a successful experiment is **experimental methodology.** While this book does not focus on this component (you'll probably take other courses focusing on experimental methodology), it is important to be aware of what good experimental methodology involves.

Controlling for Confounding Influences

To investigate the influence of a particular effect, it is critically important to keep all other potential influences constant. That is, the only influence on the effect variance should be the effect under study. For example, in an experiment to test whether the hearing of older people is different from that of younger people, the background noise should be strictly controlled. It should be identical for members of both groups. Testing one group in a perfectly quiet room (perfectly quiet with the exception of the sound stimulus used in the experiment) and the other group on a platform in New York's subway system would not provide a fair comparison of the groups' hearing ability. (In a different context, we'll look at a study involving background noise and the ability to hear sound stimuli later on in Chapter 7.)

In more general terms, any potential extraneous influence on the data collected should be controlled as tightly as possible and eliminated as much as possible. This requires two steps:

1. Deciding what possible sources of extraneous influence might exist

2. Deciding how best to control them (i.e., eliminate them to the degree possible)

Earlier in this chapter, we encountered the phenomenon of order effects. That is, in an experiment in which a subject has to do two (or more) tasks, will he or she do better on the first (or second) task, *despite* which task is actually given first. The experimental strategy of counter-balancing the order of task presentation is appropriate in these circumstances.

Counterbalancing task presentation, however, is only one example of good experimental methodology. If the data you are collecting might be influenced by the time of day the subject does the experiment, this must be controlled for by presenting all subjects with the experimental task(s) at the same time of day. [It is possible, of course, that "time of day" may be the effect under investigation in a particular study, in which case subjects would receive the task(s) at different times of the day. Presently, however, we are considering "time of day" as a possible extraneous factor.] Other possible extraneous factors include proximity to meals (this might affect motivation, ability to concentrate), bodily posture (particularly if the data you are collecting are physiological measures), temperature, lighting, and even how the experimenter interacts with the subjects when explaining the nature of the experiment.

It is not possible to present a comprehensive list of potential **confounding influences** or **confounding factors** here, because these will differ with every experiment. It is the experimenter's responsibility in each case to identify these confounding factors and to control for them.

Informed Consent

Subjects taking part in experiments should be told exactly what will happen during the experiment, and they must agree to take part in the study of their own free will. When a potential subject has been told what will happen, almost always by having the person read an **informed consent form** describing the study and then answering any questions, he or she is in a position to decide whether to take part in the study or not. If the person chooses to take part, he or she provides **informed consent**. This is provided in writing by signing an informed consent form, which is then also signed and dated by the experimenter. This form is kept on file.

It should be noted here that a subject who wants to stop participating in a study before his or her participation is complete *must be allowed to do so*. The fact that subjects signed the informed consent form at the start of the study does not give researchers the right to pressure or coerce them to carry on against their wishes.

Postexperimental Debriefing

Postexperimental briefing, often called simply **debriefing**, is necessary in experiments where the subject cannot be given a certain detail about the experimental design beforehand, because doing so could alter the way the subject perceives the experiment and affect his or her performance in the study.

Consider a study designed to investigate the influence of a drug on subjects' cognitive performance (we'll actually use an example like this later in the book, in Chapter 6). The drug will be given orally in tablet form. For purposes of experimental design, it is very useful in a study like this to include a second group of subjects who perform exactly the same experimental task(s) under precisely the same conditions, but who are given a **placebo** instead of the drug. A placebo is a tablet that is indistinguishable in looks from the experimental drug, but which does not possess the pharmacological characteristics of the experimental drug. It is critical in such a study that *subjects do not know during the study whether they were given the drug or the placebo.* However, once the study is over, the subjects have every right to know which compound, the drug or the placebo, they were given during the study.

In *every* experiment in which a certain piece of information about the study could not be shared with the subjects before the study, subjects have a right to full disclosure after the end of the study. This information is shared in individual debriefing sessions (one per subject), in which the subjects should be given every opportunity to ask any questions they would like to.

Rights of Experimental Subjects

It is important to note here that we need to have a legitimate experimental reason to consider conducting a study in which the subjects cannot be given a certain detail about the experimental design during the informed consent procedure. The reason must be that the study is addressing an important issue, and informative answers cannot be obtained if full disclosure is provided to subjects before the study commences. In almost all real-life cases where this is so, universities (and other organizations conducting experiments) will require that a document detailing the proposed study be reviewed by an oversight committee, often called an **internal review board (IRB)** or something similar. In fact, many funding agencies now require that all proposals be reviewed by an IRB before potential funding is awarded. One important aspect of the IRB's role is to protect the safety and rights of the subjects.

When conducting research, our primary concern must be the safety and the rights of our subjects. First, we must not place them in danger by asking them to do tasks that are unsafe. Second, we must at all times respect their rights. We have already discussed subjects' rights to terminate their participation at any stage of a study. They also have the right to be treated with respect and with dignity at all stages of the experiment, that is, from their **recruitment** to participate in the study right through to the end of their participation.

KEY CONCEPTS

Good Experimental Methodology

Good experimental methodology includes paying attention to:
　Controlling for Confounding Influences
　Informed Consent
　Postexperimental Debriefing
　Rights of Experimental Subjects

Design, Methodology, and Analysis

Following this brief overview of experimental methodology, we can now modify Figure 1.2 to show that experimental methodology is also important. This modification is shown in Figure 1.3. We need to do a lot of thinking before we run our experiments. Before we test the first subject in an experiment, we need to do four things:

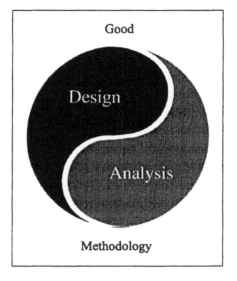

Figure 1.3.   Importance of good experimental methodology.

1. Formulate the precise research question(s) that we wish to investigate (ask).

2. Design our experiment in such a way that it is capable of providing answers.

3. Work out the appropriate experimental methodology, that is, the way we actually go about implementing our design and running our experiment.

4. Decide upon the statistical analyses that we shall use to analyze the data we collect.

However, as you've probably noticed, items 2 and 4 are really the same thing. As we've emphasized in this chapter, experimental design and analysis are inseparably linked together. The analysis we want to conduct determines our design, and once the experiment has been designed and run that way, the data must be analyzed that way. So, this list can be shortened to three items to be done before running an experiment:

1. Formulate the precise research question(s) that we wish to investigate (ask).

2. Design our experiment in such a way that it is capable of providing answers to our questions when the data collected are analyzed by the associated analysis.

3. Work out the appropriate experimental methodology, that is, the way we actually go about implementing our design and running our experiment.

In this book, we'll focus only on the first two items in this list. This certainly does not mean that the third is any less important, just that this particular book focuses on design and analysis. If you are reading this book in a class as part of a course, you might want to discuss the third item during class periods for all of the worked examples that we present.

Looking Ahead to the Following Chapters

In the next few chapters, several statistical terms and techniques will be introduced. The "mechanics" of calculating five different ANOVAs will be explained, and worked examples will be provided for each one. However, we also hope to convey a "feel" for what the analyses are doing. In this way, you will develop a sense of statistics, instead of simply obtaining a result without really knowing how or why. This feeling is particularly important if you eventually run experiments and then analyze your data using a computer. The computer will provide the mathematical results of the analyses, but you will need to **interpret** the results in the context of your study and then decide upon their importance (we'll talk about interpretation of results a lot in the following chapters).

Getting a feel for statistics is an extremely useful skill to acquire. This is true not only for conducting behavioral science research, but also in everyday life. We are constantly bombarded with "statistics" by the media. All sorts of data and figures are presented in an attempt to make us believe that this car is better than that car, or that one candidate's record is more impressive than another's (we'll get into this topic in more detail in the final chapter). We can assure you that not all of these presentations would hold up to close statistical scrutiny! A feel for the correct and appropriate application of statistics can be a big help in deciding just what and whom to believe in all sorts of situations.

MEANS, VARIANCES, SUMS OF SQUARES, AND DEGREES OF FREEDOM

As we noted in the previous chapter, for any group of scores there are two useful statistics: one describing the central value and the other describing how spread out around the central value the scores are. In the present chapter, we'll look at these in more detail.

Central Tendency

There are three common measures of central tendency:

1. The **mode** is the most frequently occurring value.

2. The **median** is a value such that equal numbers of observations lie above and below it. For any odd number of observations (e.g., 9), this is straightforward (it's the fifth number). For an even number of observations (e.g., 10), we take the average of the middle two observations (the fifth and sixth numbers).

3. As we saw in the previous chapter, the **arithmetic mean** is the sum of all the observations divided by the number of observations. In the preceding example, when calculating the median of 10 observations, it is the arithmetic mean of the fifth and sixth observations that constitutes the median. (Other types of means, e.g., the geometric mean, can be calculated. However, we shall not need to discuss any other type of mean here.)

In this book, we shall focus on the third of these measures of central tendency, the mean.

Mean

The mean is a widely used and easily calculated statistic. In describing how statistical quantities are calculated, some mathematical notation is useful. The notation used in this book will be kept to a minimum. However, certain symbols will save writing things out in full all the time. Some useful symbols right now are:

X: This refers to the scores in a particular group. A score is simply an item of information.

$\overline{X}$:   This is the mean of the group.

$\sum$:   This is an enhanced version of the Greek letter Sigma, and it is used as an instruction to add up, or sum, all the scores in the group. Thus, $\sum$ is a summation instruction.

$\sum X$:   This, therefore, is the sum of all the scores in a group.

n: This is the number of scores in a group.

So, our definition of the mean as "the sum of all the observations divided by the number of observations" can be written much more easily in notation form as

$$\overline{X} = \frac{\sum X}{n}.$$

KEY CONCEPTS

Mean

The mean of a group of scores, represented as $\overline{X}$, is calculated by the formula

$$\overline{X} = \frac{\sum X}{n}$$

Spread

The spread or dispersion of scores around the mean is another important characteristic of a group of numbers or scores. Measures of this characteristic are measures of variation.

The simplest of these measures is the range, a term we encountered in the previous chapter. This, you'll recall, is simply the arithmetic difference between the largest and the smallest value in our group of scores. However, while this measure was very useful in making a point in Figure 1.1, the range is only a rough guide to the amount of variation present. Because it only takes into account two scores from a group, it utilizes only part of the available information. Imagine a group of 100 numbers; the range would ignore 98 of them. Therefore, the range wouldn't take into account where most of the scores actually fall in the group. That is, are they close to the limits of the group as defined by the upper and lower values of the range, or are most of them nearer the middle? So, we need a better measure. Two much better measures are the **variance**, symbolically represented by s^2, and the standard deviation, symbolically represented by s.

Variance

When discussing the limitations of the range as a measure of variation, we noted that it only takes into account the largest and smallest scores in a group. It therefore provides a measure of the total spread of the group, but it does not tell us where all the rest of the scores fall within this range. In particular, it tells us nothing about how close the rest of the scores fall to a central measure of the group. So, let's think of a strategy that will tell us something about how close each score (including the two that define the range) falls to the mean. Let's try the following strategy.

Imagine the following group of scores:

6   8   10   12   14

Let's calculate the mean:

$$\overline{X} = \frac{\sum X}{n} = \frac{50}{5} = 10.$$

Now let's look at how different from the mean (or how far away from the mean) each number is. The **deviation** of each score from the mean is calculated by subtracting the mean from the score. For the first score, 6, the deviation is therefore $(6 - 10) = -4$. The five deviations are as follows:

−4   −2   0   2   4

Now let's add up all these deviations to get a total deviation:

$$(-4) + (-2) + 0 + 2 + 4 = (-6) + 0 + 6 = 0.$$

So, the total deviation of all the scores from the mean is 0 in this example.

Actually, this is not only true for this example. *The sum of the deviations of any set of scores from its mean is always equal to 0.* No matter how the scores are scattered around the mean, there will always be at least one score above the mean and at least one score below the mean (unless every score in the group is identical, in which case all the scores will be equal to the mean). Furthermore, the total negative deviation will always equal the total positive deviation, leading to a sum of all deviations equal to 0. So, this strategy isn't too much help.

Sum of Squares

However, if we take things one step further, we arrive at a very useful strategy. The next step is to *square the deviations and then add up all the resulting values.* When we do this, any negative signs become positive, because a negative number multiplied by another negative number (in this case, by itself) gives a positive answer. Therefore, when we add up all of the squared deviations, we get a positive total. (This will always be true unless all the scores are identical. In that case, all the deviations and all the squared deviations will be 0, an indication that there is no variation in the group.)

So, let's calculate the squares of the deviations in the example we used previously and add up these values. In notation form, let us calculate $\sum(X - \overline{X})^2$. So, we simply take each number, subtract the mean, square the result, and then add up the resultant values:

$$\sum(X - \overline{X})^2 = (-4)^2 + (-2)^2 + 0^2 + 2^2 + 4^2$$
$$= 16 + 4 + 0 + 4 + 16$$
$$= 40.$$

This value $\sum(X - \overline{X})^2$ is common and important in statistical analyses. It is called the **sum of squares**, or **SS**.

Like the range, the sum of squares provides a measure of dispersion or spread. However, for the reasons noted earlier, the sum of squares is a much more meaningful index. If most of the scores in a group tend to be close to the mean, the sum of squares will be relatively small. If most of them tend to be near the ends of the range, that is, relatively far away from the mean, the sum of squares will be relatively large. It is therefore possible to have two groups of scores that have identical means and identical ranges and yet yield very different sums of squares.

KEY CONCEPTS

Sum of Squares

The sum of squares (SS) is calculated by the formula

$$SS = \sum(X - \overline{X})^2$$

Variance

Once we have calculated the sum of squares, we only have to do one more thing to calculate the variance. We divide the sum of squares by the value that is one less than the number of scores in the group:

$$\text{Variance (or } s^2) = \frac{\sum(X - \overline{X})^2}{n - 1}.$$

Where does the quantity $n - 1$ come from? This value is known as the **degrees of freedom**, denoted as **df**. We'll discuss degrees of freedom next.

Degrees of Freedom

Suppose we say to you: "Choose any five numbers that add up to 100." How much choice do you actually have? A few moments' thought will show you that you can only choose four numbers; you will have no choice about the fifth. (You can, of course, choose many different sets of four numbers, but you have no choice at all concerning the fifth on any of these occasions.) Suppose you choose 27, 9, 6, and 30. Your fifth choice *must be* 28. Or, say you choose 43, 31, 19, and 25. (These total more than 100, so the fifth number must be negative.) This time your choice must be −18. In other words, there are four degrees of freedom to your choice; four choices have freedom, the fifth does not.

Now, imagine that the previous question, "Choose any five numbers that add up to 100," is expressed in a slightly different way, but a way that actually amounts to *exactly the same thing*. That is, "Choose any five numbers that have a mean of 20." This is the same thing because any five numbers that add up to 100 will have a mean of 20. Once again, therefore, you will find that while you can choose the first four numbers, you have no choice in picking your fifth. Thus, *in a group of scores with a fixed mean, there is one less degree of freedom than the total number of scores.*

For those of you who like more mathematical definitions, the degrees of freedom may be defined as the number of squares minus the number of independent linear restrictions placed upon the quantities involved. For n numbers, there are n squares of deviations from the mean, of which only $n - 1$ are independent. When $n - 1$ are specified, the nth is also determined.

We should note here that, although the term $n - 1$ is used by the vast majority of textbooks, including this one, it is possible that you may occasionally see n used as the denominator when calculating variance. For theoretical reasons, the version used here is better. We will not explain these reasons in great detail here, but you can think of it this way. Each time we run an experiment, we use a certain number of subjects. For example, we discussed using 20 racing car drivers in a reaction time experiment in Chapter 1. These 20 subjects are a **sample** of the total **population** of all racing car drivers. While our experiment and our statistical analyses will actually give us answers about that specific sample of racing car drivers, what we are really trying to discover is information that will be applicable for (i.e., information that will generalize to) all racing car drivers. The best way to do this is to use $n - 1$ as the denominator. While use of n as the denominator will give the precise variance for that particular randomly chosen sample of 20 drivers, the best estimate of the population variance is given by the use of $n - 1$.

An Easier Method of Calculating Variance

The method of calculating variance just presented was used because it explicitly captures the nature of the calculation. That is, it captures the fact that we have to calculate each deviation about the mean, square it, find the sum of squares, and divide by the degrees of freedom. However, if we have a large group of scores, doing all these steps takes a lot of time. Fortunately, there is an easier method of calculating variance:

1. Square each score and add up all the values. That is, calculate the sum of the squares of the individual scores.

2. Add up all the scores and square the total. Then divide this value by the number of scores.

3. Subtract the answer in Step 2 from the answer in Step 1.

4. Divide the answer in Step 3 by $n - 1$.

This process is represented in notation form by the following formula:

$$s^2 = \frac{\sum X^2 - (\sum X)^2/n}{n - 1}.$$

In words, this formula can be expressed as "Variance equals the sum of the squares of the individual scores minus the square of the total of the scores divided by n, all divided by the degrees of freedom." The notation $\sum X^2$ is expressed in words as "Sigma X squared." This is Step 1. The notation $(\sum X)^2$ is expressed in words as "Sigma X all squared." What this means is "find $\sum X$ and square this value." This is the first part of Step 2.

It is important to note here that $\sum X^2$, "Sigma X squared," is quite different from $(\sum X)^2$, "Sigma X all squared," even though they look and sound rather similar at first. However, as you learn about the different types of analyses in the following chapters, you will become very familiar with both of these terms, and any initial confusion will quickly disappear.

Correction Factor

The last part of the top of this new equation for calculating variance, $(\sum X)^2/n$, is called the **correction factor**. This part "corrects" the whole top line (the **numerator)** of the equation so that the calculated value of the numerator becomes exactly equal to $\sum(X - \overline{X})^2$, the sum of the squared deviations, which, as we saw in the initial formula for calculating variance, is what we actually need as the numerator. The advantage of the second formula is that, particularly as our groups of scores become larger, the two terms $\sum X^2$ and $(\sum X)^2/n$ are much easier to calculate by hand than the term $\sum(X - \overline{X})^2$.

Calculating Variance Both Ways

To demonstrate how both methods work, let's use both formulas on the set of scores we used previously. The scores were:

6   8   10   12   14

Let's calculate the variance using each method:

Method 1

Scores	Deviations from Mean	Squared Deviations
6	−4	16
8	−2	4
10	0	0
12	2	4
14	4	16

$\sum X = 50,$

$n = 5,$

$\overline{X} = 10.$

$\sum(X - \overline{X})^2 = 40,$

$$\frac{\sum(X - \overline{X})^2}{n-1} = \frac{40}{4} = 10.$$

So, these scores have a mean of 10 and, coincidentally, a variance of 10.

Method 2

1.

$$\sum X^2 = 6^2 + 8^2 + 10^2 + 12^2 + 14^2$$
$$= 36 + 64 + 100 + 144 + 196$$
$$= 540.$$

2.

$$\left(\sum X\right)^2 = (6 + 8 + 10 + 12 + 14)^2$$
$$= 50^2$$
$$= 2500.$$

3.

$$\frac{(\sum X)^2}{n} = \frac{2500}{5} = 500.$$

4.

$$\frac{\sum X^2 - (\sum X)^2}{n-1} = \frac{540 - 500}{4} = \frac{40}{4} = 10.$$

While the first method is very useful because it explains the rationale behind our calculations, in practice, the second method is usually used.

KEY CONCEPTS

Variance

Variance can be calculated by two formulas, both of which give the same answer. In practice, the second one is usually used.

$$s^2 = \frac{\sum(X - \overline{X})^2}{n-1}$$

and

$$s^2 = \frac{\sum X^2 - (\sum X)^2/n}{n-1}$$

Standard Deviation

The last term we'll introduce in this chapter is the **standard deviation**, which is represented in notation form as **SD**. The standard deviation is simply the square root of the variance. Once the variance of a group of scores has been found, calculating the standard deviation is a one-step process. So, for our set of scores,

$$SD = \sqrt{10} = 3.162.$$

This measure of variation is used very frequently. It has one big advantage over variance: *Its units are those of the original scores.* What do we mean by this? In all of our experiments, all of our scores are not simply numbers, they are actually measures of something. Therefore, they have **units**. The scores may be reaction times, in which case the unit of measurement would be "hundredths of a second." They may be measures of heart rate, in which case they would have the units "beats per minute." Because the calculation of variance involves squaring, the variance of a set of reaction time scores has as its unit "squared hundredths of a second." Similarly, the variance of a set of heart rates has as its unit "squared beats per minute." So, the process of squaring data, which proves so useful in circumventing the problem of zero total deviations discussed earlier, actually creates another potential problem. That is, the units of our measure of variance are not the same as the units of the scores (data) we started with.

Fortunately, this problem can be solved very easily by taking the square root of the variance, that is, by calculating the standard deviation. This process returns the units of measurement to the units used originally in collecting our data.

KEY CONCEPTS

Standard Deviation

The standard deviation (s) is the square root of the variance (s^2).

SUMMARY

In this chapter, we have become familiar with some key components of statistical analysis: means, standard deviations, sums of squares, and degrees of freedom. We are now ready to look at ANOVAs themselves.

INDEPENDENT-GROUPS ANALYSIS OF VARIANCE

ONE-FACTOR INDEPENDENT-GROUPS ANALYSIS OF VARIANCE

When we are interested in investigating just one source of influence, or effect, on our data, a **one-factor ANOVA** is the appropriate design to use. In one-factor ANOVAs, we compare the variance due to the effect under investigation with the variance due to chance. That is, we compare the effect variance with the error variance. As we saw in Chapter 1, a simple way to compare two such values is to form a ratio, dividing one variance by the other.

F Test

The statistical test used to do this is called the **F test**, after the statistician R. A. Fisher who developed it. Therefore,

$$F = \frac{\text{Effect Variance}}{\text{Error Variance}}.$$

In our ANOVAs, F has to reach a certain size to attain statistical significance. This size is dictated by the degrees of freedom applicable in each instance. These values are given in the **tables of critical values of F**, which appear in Appendix A. To attain significance, F must always be greater than 1, and often considerably greater. We'll explain this more thoroughly as we work through an example in a few moments.

Assumptions Underlying Our Statistical Tests

For our statistical tests to be valid, several assumptions have been incorporated into the formulas. Three assumptions are common to most statistical tests, including the F test. The first assumption is that the observations are independent. That is to say, each observation is uncorrelated with any other observation. A second assumption is that the observations are normally distributed. This means that all of the measures of central tendency of the observed scores, the mean, the median, and the mode, would be the same. The third assumption is that the variances are the same. That is, our measures of spread of the scores have to be identical. This assumption is often called homogeneity of variances.

The first assumption, of independence, is very important. When this assumption is violated, the results of our tests can be very misleading. We will see this later when we discuss repeated-measures designs where each subject contributes more that one score each. In general, our statistical tests are reasonably immune to violations of the latter two assumptions when they occur alone. However, when they occur together, our tests can be very biased and special techniques have been developed to deal with those situations.

Worked Example

In this chapter, and in Chapters 4 through 7, we'll work through an example, showing you how to calculate all the necessary terms to complete the ANOVA. We'll also explain why we do what we do.

TABLE 3.1 Marks for Undergraduates, Graduates, and Professors		
Undergraduates	Graduates	Professors
6	8	10
5	9	8
6	8	10
7	9	8
6	6	9

Here is the research question. Five undergraduate students, five graduate students, and five professors were given a statistics test. The marks attained out of a possible 10 are given in Table 3.1. Did the groups differ in how well they did on the test?

Before we start to do any mathematical calculations, let's think about the question in terms of the effect under study. To decide what the effect under study is, we look at the three groups and see what makes them different from each other. That is, what distinguishes the members of one group from the members of all other groups? Well, the three groups of subjects belong to three easily identifiable positions within university life: undergraduates, graduate students, and professors. Let's summarize this categorization as "University Position." The effect we are studying, therefore, is University Position. This is the **factor** under investigation in this experiment. In this experiment, we have three different groups of subjects who are part of our factor University Position. These are referred to as the three **levels** of the factor.

(By the way, we don't *have* to use the phrase "University Position." You can use any phrase you like that captures the meaning of the experiment. Another possibility might be "Years of Study." You can probably think of others, too.)

Now let's see how we work through this one-factor ANOVA. The calculations needed are as follows:

Group Totals and the Grand Total

First, we calculate the **total scores**, that is, the **group totals** and the **grand total**. The totals are as follow:

$$\text{Undergraduates} = 30,$$
$$\text{Graduates} = 40,$$
$$\text{Professors} = 45,$$
$$\text{Grand Total} = 115. \ (\text{This is } 30 + 40 + 45.)$$

Group Means and the Grand Mean

Next, we calculate the **group means** and the overall mean, called the **grand mean**:

$$\text{Undergraduate Group Mean} = \frac{6 + 5 + 6 + 7 + 6}{5} = \frac{30}{5} = 6,$$

$$\text{Graduate Group Mean} = \frac{40}{5} = 8,$$

$$\text{Professor Group Mean} = \frac{45}{5} = 9,$$

$$\text{Grand Mean} = \frac{6 + 8 + 9}{3} = 7.67.$$

KEY CONCEPTS

The steps in a one-factor independent-groups ANOVA involve calculating:

Group Totals and the Grand Total
Group Means and the Grand Mean
Correction Factor
Total Sum of Squares
Between-Groups Sum of Squares
Within-Groups Sum of Squares
Degrees of Freedom
Mean Squares
F Value
p Value

Correction Factor

Calculate the correction factor, CF. This is simply the square of the grand total divided by the total number of scores:

$$CF = \frac{(\sum X)^2}{n} = \frac{115^2}{15} = \frac{13225}{15} = 881.67.$$

Total Sum of Squares

Calculate the total sum of squares (SS). This is done by adding up the squares of the scores and subtracting the correction factor:

$$\begin{aligned} \text{Total SS} &= \sum X^2 - \text{CF} \\ &= 917 - 881.67 \\ &= 35.33. \end{aligned}$$

Between-Groups Sum of Squares

Calculate the between-groups sum of squares. This is done by taking each group total, squaring it, dividing each answer by the number in each group, adding these numbers, and subtracting the correction factor. This sounds *much* worse than it is: In symbol form, it looks much easier:

Group Totals:	30	40	45
(Group Totals)^2:	900	1600	2025
$\frac{(\text{Group Totals})^2}{n}$:	$\frac{900}{n}$	$\frac{1600}{n}$	$\frac{2025}{n}$
	$= 180$	320	405.

So,

$$180 + 320 + 405 - \text{CF} = 905 - 881.67 = 23.33.$$

Within-Groups Sum of Squares

Calculate the within-groups sum of squares. This step doesn't need to be calculated directly; it can be found by subtraction. The breakdown, or **partitioning**, of variance for this type of ANOVA is shown

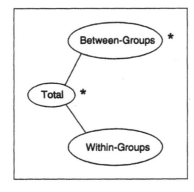

Figure 3.1. Variance breakdown for one-factor independent-groups ANOVA.

in the "Bubble Diagram" in Figure 3.1. The asterisks show the SS values we have already calculated. So, the within-groups SS can be found by subtracting the between-groups SS from the total SS. Therefore,

$$\text{Within-Groups SS} = \text{Total SS} - \text{Between-Groups SS}$$
$$= 35.33 - 23.33$$
$$= 12.$$

Degrees of Freedom

We now need the degrees of freedom for each previous step.

▶ *Total*: We started with 15 scores. To get the same grand total, 14 of these can vary, but the 15th cannot. So, we have $n - 1$ degrees of freedom here:

$$\text{df} = 15 - 1 = 14.$$

▶ *Between Groups*: There are three groups and, thus, three group totals. These must also add up to the grand total. So, once two have been found, the other cannot vary. Again, then, there are $n - 1$ degrees of freedom:

$$\text{df} = 3 - 1 = 2.$$

▶ *Within Groups*: By exactly the same logic that we saw for the SS values (see Within-Groups Sum of Squares), we can calculate these degrees of freedom as

$$df(\text{Within Groups}) = df(\text{Total}) - df(\text{Between Groups})$$
$$= 14 - 2 = 12.$$

(*There is another way to think of this. We are dealing here within groups; so, let us work out the df within each group. There are five scores for each group. So, df = 4 per group. There are three groups. The total within-groups df is the total dfs within each group, = 4 + 4 + 4 = 12.*)

ANOVA SUMMARY TABLE ◀

We have now done all the calculations we need to do using the original scores and the breakdown diagrams. The values of interest now go into an **analysis of variance summary table,** shown in Table 3.2.

We have three more steps to complete our analysis.

KEY CONCEPTS

The five items that go in an ANOVA summary table, along with the sources of variance, are:

Sum of Squares (SS)
Degrees of Freedom (df)
Mean Squares (MS)
F Value
p Value

TABLE 3.2 Initial ANOVA Summary Table

Source	SS	df	MS	F	p
Between Groups	35.33	2			
Within Groups	12.00	12			

Calculation of Mean Squares

Mean squares (MS) are calculated by dividing each sum of squares by the associated df:

$$\text{Between-Groups MS} = \frac{35.33}{2} = 17.67,$$

$$\text{Within-Groups MS} = \frac{12.0}{12} = 1.0.$$

Calculation of F

The F ratio is calculated as the between-groups MS divided by the within-groups MS:

$$F = \frac{17.67}{1.0} = 17.67.$$

p Level

The last step involves finding the level of statistical significance that the F value obtained. There are always *two* df values associated with an F value. The first is the df value associated with the numerator of the F ratio. The second is the df value associated with the **denominator** of the F ratio. In this case, the numerator is between-group, and the df value associated with this is 2. The denominator is within-group, and the df value associated with that is 12. So

$$F(2, 12) = 17.67.$$

F tables are used to determine the significance of such a result. If you look at the set of F tables in Appendix A, you will see that the degrees of freedom for the numerator are arranged along the top of the page, and the degrees of freedom for the denominator down the page. We want $F(2, 12)$. We first check the 5% table. A value of 3.88 will be found. Our result was 17.67, which does attain significance at the 5% (0.05) level. We can therefore proceed to check out the more significant

TABLE 3.3	**Completed ANOVA Summary Table**				
Source	SS	df	MS	F	p
Between Groups	35.33	2	17.67	17.67	< 0.01
Within Groups	12.00	12	1.00		

1% (0.01) level. A value of 6.93 will be found. Our result of 17.67 also attains statistical significance at the 1% level.

We can now complete the ANOVA summary table, as shown in Table 3.3.

Interpreting Our Results

The final step is to **interpret** the data. Our statistical tests will alw give us a mathematically correct view of the data, which then ne to be expressed in the context of the research question. This particular analysis, the one-factor independent-groups ANOVA, provides just one F value. The "mathematical" answer from our analysis is

$$F(2,12) = 17.67, \qquad p < 0.01.$$

It is now up to us to interpret the mathematical answer by referring back to the original question we set out to answer.

KEY CONCEPTS

Interpretation, Interpretation, Interpretation!

You've probably heard the old statement that the most important considerations when buying a house are location, location, and location. This statement is used to emphasize the paramount importance of this consideration. In terms of using statistical analyses to answer research questions, a similar concept applies: Correct and appropriate interpretation of our mathematical results is of paramount importance.

The original research question was: Do the groups of subjects (undergraduates, graduates, and professors) differ in how well they did on the test? We decided that we would call the factor under investigation University Position. We interpret our result in the following manner:

1. We have evidence at the 1% level that the levels of the factor University Position differ. Therefore, *there is a statistically significant difference in performance on the test among the groups.*

2. The preceding statement, by itself, does not tell us anything about which group performed best, second best, and worst. Next, therefore, we look at the means for each group. We calculated these in the second step of the analysis (see Group Means and the Grand Mean). These means are:

Undergraduates = 6,   Graduates = 8,   Professors = 9.

So, graduates performed better than undergraduates, and professors performed better than graduates.

Multiple Comparisons

Interestingly, we still do not have a full answer to our question. We now know the relative performance of the three groups, and we know that the groups differed significantly, but *we do not know how the groups differed significantly.* There are a number of possibilities:

▶ All groups performed significantly differently from each other.

▶ The professors performed significantly better than both the graduates and the undergraduates, while the graduates and the undergraduates did not differ significantly in performance from each other.

▶ The professors and the graduates both performed significantly better than the undergraduates, but did not differ significantly in performance from each other.

▶ The professors and the undergraduates differed significantly in performance from each other, while neither group differed significantly in performance from the graduates.

▶ None of the individual groups differed significantly from each other.

To decide which possibility occurred here, we need an additional analysis.

In situations such as this, where we have a partial answer to our original research question, **multiple comparisons** are performed. These are tests that allow us to compare means, or groups of means, to get a more detailed understanding of our data than is provided by the overall (or what are called **omnibus**) tests produced by the ANOVA.

A multiple-comparison strategy that is appropriate here is the use of the **independent-groups *t* test**. (We'll discuss another type of *t* test in Chapter 5.) The independent-groups *t* test, sometimes called the *t* test for a difference between two independent means, compares two sets of scores from two independent groups of subjects and allows us to determine whether the means of the groups are statistically significant. Because the groups are independent, this *t* test can handle situations in which there are different numbers of observations in the two groups. First, therefore, we'll present an example using two groups of scores, A and B, containing different numbers of scores. Then, we'll return to the current worked example concerning the undergraduates, graduates, and professors.

KEY CONCEPTS

Independent-Groups *t* Test

This test is useful for conducting multiple comparisons when the factor of interest has more than two levels.

Example of the Independent-Groups t Test

Imagine two groups of numbers, called Group A and Group B. The number of scores in A is represented as N_A, and the number of scores in B is represented as N_B. The following calculations are needed:

1. Calculate X_A, $\overline{X}_A$, $\sum X_A$, $(\sum X_A)^2$, and $\sum X_A^2$.

2. Calculate X_B, $\overline{X}_B$, $\sum X_B$, $(\sum X_B)^2$, and $\sum X_B^2$.

3. Calculate $\sum X_A^2 - (\sum X_A)^2 / N_A$.

4. Calculate $\sum X_B^2 - (\sum X_B)^2 / N_B$.

Now, we substitute these calculated values into the following equation:

$$t = \frac{\overline{X}_A - \overline{X}_B}{\sqrt{\left[\dfrac{\sum X_A^2 - \dfrac{(\sum X_A)^2}{N_A} + \sum X_B^2 - \dfrac{(\sum X_B)^2}{N_B}}{(N_A + N_B) - 2}\right]\left[\dfrac{1}{N_A} + \dfrac{1}{N_B}\right]}}.$$

This formula is not anywhere near as daunting as it appears at first sight. Let's go through an example to see how it works. Here are our two groups, A and B:

Group A ($N = 8$): 7, 6, 4, 7, 6, 5, 8, 5,

Group B ($N = 10$): 9, 9, 10, 8, 9, 10, 9, 8, 10, 11.

Here are the calculations:

	Group A	Group B
X	48.0	93.0
$\overline{X}$	6.0	9.3
$\sum X^2$	300.0	873.0
$\dfrac{(\sum X)^2}{N}$	288.0	864.9

We now substitute these values into the equation as follows:

$$t = \frac{6 - 9.3}{\sqrt{\left[\dfrac{300 - 288 + 873 - 864.9}{16}\right]\left[\dfrac{1}{8} + \dfrac{1}{10}\right]}}$$

$$= -6.13.$$

The minus sign here at the end is not important, because had we labeled groups A and B the other way around, the answer would have been +6.13. So, it is simply the *magnitude* of the t value that is important.

Degrees of Freedom

To check the significance of the t test result, we need to know the associated degrees of freedom. These are the total of the degrees of freedom in A plus the degrees of freedom in B. That is,

$$df = (N_A - 1) + (N_B - 1).$$

This can be written in a more elegant (mathematically equivalent) way as

$$df = (N_A + N_B) - 2.$$

This expression of the degrees of freedom appeared in the basic equation for calculating the t value.

In our example, then,

$$\begin{aligned} df &= (8 + 10) - 2 \\ &= 18 - 2 \\ &= 16. \end{aligned}$$

Therefore,

$$t(16) = 6.13.$$

Tables of Critical Values of the *t* Distribution

In the same manner as we have already seen for F tests, there are tables of critical values for t tests. These are presented in Appendix B. As for F values, we check out the 5% table first. Our result attains significance at the 5% level. So, we can proceed to check out the result at the 1% level. Our result also obtains significance at the 1% level.

So, there is statistically significant evidence at the 1% level of a difference between the group means. We now look at the actual means to determine which is larger. From our earlier calculations, the mean of A is 6.0 and the mean of B is 9.3. Therefore, the Group B mean is significantly larger.

Back to This Chapter's Worked Example

In this chapter's worked example, you'll remember that we have three groups, undergraduates, graduates, and professors. To find out how the groups differ significantly, we can perform three comparisons using independent-groups t tests:

1. Compare the undergraduates and graduates.

2. Compare the graduates and professors.

3. Compare the undergraduates and professors.

If you work through the three t tests following the method described previously, you will see that the results for these comparisons are as follows:

$$\text{Comparison 1:} \quad t(8) = 3.16, \quad p < 0.05,$$
$$\text{Comparison 2:} \quad t(8) = 1.41, \quad \text{ns,}$$
$$\text{Comparison 3:} \quad t(8) = 5.48, \quad p < 0.01.$$

Now that we have the mathematical answers from the multiple comparisons, we need to interpret them in the context of our experiment.

We'll also use the group means that we've already calculated. Our interpretation is as follows:

1. There is evidence at the 5% level that graduate students performed significantly better than undergraduates.

2. There is no evidence that graduate students and professors performed significantly differently.

3. There is evidence at the 1% level that professors performed significantly better than undergraduates.

We deliberately used three levels in this worked example to demonstrate how multiple comparisons are conducted. Multiple comparisons are not needed when there are only two levels. If a significant F value is obtained in a one-factor ANOVA when there are only two levels, there is only one possible interpretation: *The two levels differ significantly from each other*. The group means tell you the direction of the significant difference.

An Interesting Question Concerning One-Factor Independent-Groups ANOVAs and Independent-Groups *t* Tests

At this point, you may be asking yourself a very reasonable question: Because we needed *t* tests after our one-factor ANOVA to get a complete answer to our research question, could we simply have conducted the three *t* tests in the first place instead of performing the ANOVA? In other words, can the independent-groups *t* test strategy be used in place of the independent one-factor ANOVA design?

The answer is yes it can. In cases where there are only two levels, only one *t* test is needed (all we can do is compare the first level with the second). The *t* test and the one-factor ANOVA will give *precisely the same answer in terms of the degree of statistical significance obtained*. The actual *t* value and F value will not be the same (in fact, the F value is the square of the t value in the two-level case), but the associated p values will be identical. When there are more than two levels, more than one t test is needed, one for each possible comparison between pairs of levels. If one knows in advance what comparisons are of interest, the multiple-comparison approach using t tests may be more appropriate.

However, there is a definite two-part advantage in studying the one-factor ANOVA design when more than two levels are present. First, if one does not have any prior ideas about which comparisons are of interest, the one-factor ANOVA design provides a very efficient way to test for differences among the groups. Second, an understanding of this design is a big help in understanding the two-factor ANOVA design discussed in the next chapter. While some of the computational details vary from the one-factor design to the two-factor design, there is a logical conceptual progression, and therefore familiarity with the one-factor design pays off handsomely.

SUMMARY

In this chapter, we introduced the one-factor independent-groups ANOVA. We explained when it is appropriate to use this design, and showed how to perform all the necessary steps required by the analysis. We explained this process in detail because, although some of the individual calculation steps in the other ANOVAs will be different, the general principles behind all the ANOVAs are similar. The topic of multiple comparisons was also introduced. The independent-groups t test is useful when the factor of interest has more than two levels.

EXERCISES

Here, and at the end of each of the next four chapters, two exercises are given. The first requires you to interpret the results of an ANOVA (the type of ANOVA discussed in the respective chapter). The second exercise requires you to conduct an ANOVA and then provide an interpretation. Answers to all exercises are provided in Appendix C at the end of the book.

1. The number of sick days of a group of workers from Factory Q and a group of workers from Factory R were compared using a one-factor independent-groups ANOVA. The average number of sick days for each factory were 12.7 and 15.1, respectively. The ANOVA results were: $F(1, 60) = 3.26$, $p = \text{ns}$. Provide a full interpretation of the results.

2. Groups A and B did a time estimation experiment. Their results are as follows:

Group A	*Group B*
24	36
35	42
39	51
43	59
50	65

Perform a one-factor independent-groups ANOVA and provide a full interpretation of the results.

TWO-FACTOR INDEPENDENT-GROUPS ANALYSIS OF VARIANCE

While the one-factor ANOVA is very useful in some situations, its name indicates a limitation: It is designed for (and, from what we've seen about design and analysis, it can analyze) those situations involving just one source of variance. In many cases, we want to look at two (or more) sources of variation simultaneously. A two-factor design means that two sources of variance can be investigated in a single experiment. It also means that the **interaction** between two sources (i.e., two factors) can be investigated. We'll discuss what is meant by the term interaction effect later in this chapter. The investigation of the interaction between factors is not possible if we do two experiments, each of which examines one of the two factors.

In a two-factor ANOVA, we get three F values of interest. Call the Factors A and B (there is no particular reason for these letters). We get F values for

1. Factor A main effect

2. Factor B main effect

3. The A × B interaction

The word **main**, like the word significant, is used here in a statistical context. It refers to the effect of that particular factor on the measures obtained during the experiment. It does not necessarily mean the "largest" or "most important" as the word "main" does in everyday use. We noted previously that the two-factor ANOVA allows the investigation of **interactions**; it is quite possible for Factor A and Factor B to show no significant effects, that is, for both main effects to be nonsignificant, while the A × B interaction is highly significant.

KEY CONCEPTS

In a two-factor ANOVA, we get three F values:

Factor A Main Effect
Factor B Main Effect
The A × B Interaction

Interactions

What precisely do we mean by an **interaction**? Imagine an experiment designed to test two types of teaching methods, and to investigate these methods using two types of students, undergraduates and graduates. This gives us a two-factor ANOVA design:

Factor 1—Teaching Method.
    Number of Levels (Method 1 and Method 2) = 2,
Factor 2—Type of Student.
    Number of Levels (Undergraduates and Graduates) = 2.

We draw this design like this:

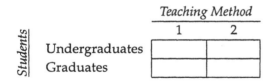

In our study, each of the two teaching methods lasts a week. Four undergraduates get Teaching Method 1, and another four undergraduates get Teaching Method 2. Similarly, four graduates get Teaching Method 1, and another four graduates get Teaching Method 2. At the end of the course, a test is given. Our experimental data (scores) will be test marks at the end of the course, and these scores will occur for every combination of the levels of both factors. That is, we get scores for undergraduates for both Methods 1 and 2, and we also get scores for graduates for both Methods 1 and 2.

Now, suppose that undergraduates do very well with Method 1, and poorly with Method 2. And suppose graduates do very well with Method 2, and poorly with Method 1. This is an example of an **interaction effect**. The factors Type of Student and Teaching Method **interact** such that they influence each other differently according to the different levels of the factors.

We shall consider interactions in more detail later. For now, simply be aware that they are an integral part of two-factor ANOVAs, not just an unwanted nuisance. Indeed, in some experiments the interaction can be the main focus of attention.

Two-Factor Independent-Groups ANOVA

In this chapter, we shall focus on the two-factor independent-groups ANOVA. In this design, the various combinations of the levels of the two factors are given to independent groups, hence the name of the design. In other words, *each subject provides only one score*. Each factor can have any number of levels greater than 1 (there must be at least two levels; otherwise, the analysis becomes a one-factor ANOVA). Let's work through an example of this kind of design.

Worked Example

We are interested in finding out how well undergraduates and graduates will learn when taught by two different teaching methods, Method 1 and Method 2. As we noted in Chapter 1, before running an experiment to investigate this issue, we need to:

1. Formulate the precise research question that we wish to investigate (ask).

2. Design our experiment in such a way that it is capable of providing answers to our question when the data collected are analyzed by the associated analysis.

Our research question in this case is: Are Methods 1 and 2 equally effective in teaching undergraduates and graduates?

We need to design an experiment that includes both types of students and both types of teaching methods. We also need to have a way of evaluating how effective the teaching method is. Giving a test at the end seems a reasonable way of doing this. An appropriate experimental design to use is the design being discussed in this chapter, the two-factor independent-groups design, the results from which will be analyzed by a two-factor independent-groups ANOVA. Let's make Factor A Type of Student. Factor A therefore has two levels, undergraduates and graduates. This means that Factor B will be Type of Teaching Method. Factor B also has two levels, Method 1 and Method 2.

Imagine, then, that we conducted this experiment. Four undergraduates were taught by Method 1, and another four undergraduates were taught by Method 2. Similarly, four graduates were taught by Method 1 and four others by Method 2. At the end of the courses, the students were given a test. The data presented in Table 4.1 are the marks obtained out of a possible 20.

Before starting our calculations, let's consider the nature of this design. We only have one score per subject, so all variance is between subjects. These subjects are broken down into groups that are defined according to both factors, which we'll call A and B. This means that we

TABLE 4.1 Experimental Data for the 16 Subjects in This Study

| | | Factor B | | |
		Method 1	Method 2	Totals
	Undergraduates	8	6	
		11	7	
		8	8	
Factor A		9	7	64
	Graduates	16	12	
		18	11	
		17	12	
		17	9	112
	Totals	104	72	176

16 subjects, one score each.

have **AB groups of subjects.** What exactly does this mean? It means that we have groups of subjects that cannot be defined by considering one factor alone. We need to consider both factors together to define these groups. What are our AB groups? There are four of them. We have an "undergraduates, Method 1" group, an "undergraduates, Method 2" group, and two similar groups for graduates. Each AB group is called a **treatment.** A treatment is a particular combination of a level of one factor and a level of another factor. Here, then, we have four treatments; "undergraduates, Method 1," "undergraduates, Method 2," "graduates, Method 1," and "graduates, Method 2."

In doing the necessary calculations for this analysis, some of them will be similar to those for the one-factor ANOVA we described in the previous chapter. Some of the calculations, however, will be different because this ANOVA has two factors. The calculations needed are as follows, and the variance breakdown diagram for this design is shown in Figure 4.1 on the next page.

Group Totals and the Grand Total

The group totals were shown in Table 4.1. The totals of 64 and 112 are the totals for undergraduates and graduates, respectively. In calculating

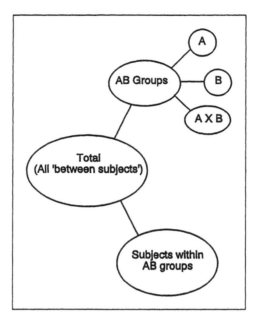

Figure 4.1. Variance breakdown for the two-factor independent-groups ANOVA.

these, *the fact that some students received Method 1 and some Method 2 is ignored temporarily.* The totals for Method 1 and Method 2 are 104 and 72, respectively. Again, in calculating these, *we temporarily ignore the fact that some scores came from undergraduates and some from graduates.*

▶ The grand total, 176, is also shown in Table 4.1. It is calculated by adding up all the scores.

▶ Unlike the one-factor ANOVA in the previous chapter, we now have to calculate totals for each treatment, that is, each AB group. We have four treatments and, hence, four totals as follows:

	Method 1	Method 2
Undergraduates	36	28
Graduates	68	44

Group Means and the Grand Mean

Now we calculate means from the totals calculated previously:

$$\text{Undergraduate Mean} = \frac{64}{8} = 8, \qquad \text{Graduate Mean} = \frac{112}{8} = 14,$$

$$\text{Method 1 Mean} = \frac{104}{8} = 13, \qquad \text{Method 2 Mean} = \frac{72}{8} = 9,$$

$$\text{Grand Mean} = \frac{176}{16} = 11.$$

The treatment means are:

	Method 1	Method 2
Undergraduates	9	7
Graduates	17	11

Correction Factor

Calculating the correction factor, CF, is done exactly as in Chapter 3. That is, divide the square of the grand total by the total number of scores:

$$CF = \frac{(\sum X)^2}{n} = \frac{30976}{16} = 1936.$$

Total Sum of Squares

This is, again, calculated as in Chapter 3. We add up all the squares of the numbers and subtract the correction factor:

$$\begin{aligned}
\text{Total SS} &= \sum X^2 - CF \\
&= 8^2 + 11^2 + \cdots + 12^2 + 9^2 - CF \\
&= 2176 - 1936 \\
&= 240.
\end{aligned}$$

Sum of Squares for Each of the Factors

We now deal with each factor in turn. We'll start with Type of Student. For this calculation, we temporarily ignore classifications made on the basis of the other factor. Type of Student has two levels, and so we have two totals. Each of these is made up of eight scores (we ignore the fact that four fall under Method 1 and four fall under Method 2 in each case). So, we square these totals, divide each result by the number of scores that made up each total, and subtract the correction factor:

$$\text{Student SS} = \frac{64^2}{8} + \frac{112^2}{8} - \text{CF}$$
$$= 2080 - 1936$$
$$= 144.$$

Now we'll deal with the other factor, Teaching Method. Again, for this calculation, we ignore classifications made on the basis of the other factor. Teaching Method has two levels, Method 1 and Method 2. There are therefore two totals, one for each level. Each is made up of eight scores (we ignore the fact that four in each case come from undergraduates and four from graduates). We square the two totals, divide each result by the number of scores that made up that total, and subtract the correction factor:

$$\text{Teaching Method SS} = \frac{104^2}{8} + \frac{72^2}{8} - \text{CF}$$
$$= 2000 - 1936$$
$$= 64.$$

Sum of Squares for the AB Treatments (AB Groups)

We now calculate the AB groups sum of squares. At this point, let's change A and B to something more meaningful in the context of this particular experiment (we don't have to do this, but it makes the example easier to follow). The factors here are Type of Student, which we'll call S, and Teaching Method, which we'll call T. So, we want to calculate the S/T treatment groups sum of squares. This is done by taking each S/T group total, squaring it, dividing each answer by the number of scores that made up that total, adding these values together, and subtracting the correction factor:

$$S/T \text{ Groups SS} = \frac{36^2}{4} + \frac{28^2}{4} + \frac{68^2}{4} + \frac{44^2}{4} - CF$$
$$= 2160 - 1936$$
$$= 224.$$

Subjects Within S/T Groups Sum of Squares

The previous calculations involved in this design are carried out directly from the data. To get the remaining SS values, we use the breakdown diagram shown in Figure 4.2. As in the previous chapter, the as-

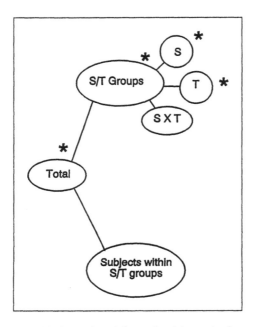

Figure 4.2. Variance breakdown for this worked example.

terisks show what can be calculated directly. The other values can be found by simple subtraction.

We can see from the breakdown diagram that:

Total SS = S/T Groups SS + Subjects Within S/T Groups SS.

Therefore,

$$\begin{aligned} \text{Subjects Within S/T Groups SS} &= \text{Total SS} - \text{S/T Groups SS} \\ &= 240 - 224 \\ &= 16. \end{aligned}$$

S × T Sum of Squares

We can see from the breakdown diagram that:

S/T Groups SS = S SS + T SS + S × T SS.

Therefore,

$$\begin{aligned} \text{S × T SS} &= \text{S/T Groups SS} - \text{S SS} - \text{T SS} \\ &= 224 - 144 - 64 \\ &= 16. \end{aligned}$$

We can see from this formula that the interaction SS (S × T SS) is what is left over from the S/T groups SS after removing the variance associated with the main effect of Student (S) and the main effect of Teaching Method (T). The interaction is always what is left over after taking into account the main effects. This is very important for our interpretation of the results, as we will see later.

Degrees of Freedom

We now need to work out the degrees of freedom for each part of the breakdown diagram.

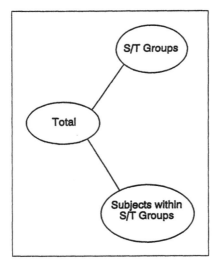

Figure 4.3. Calculating the degrees of freedom.

▶ *Total*: We have 16 scores. Therefore,

$$df = n - 1 = 16 - 1 = 15.$$

▶ S/T *Groups*: There are four S/T treatments:

$$df = n - 1 = 4 - 1 = 3.$$

▶ *Subjects Within* S/T *Groups*: Looking at the breakdown diagram shown in Figure 4.3 is helpful here. So, if there are 15 degrees of freedom for the total and there are 3 degrees of freedom for the S/T groups, then there are $15 - 3 = 12$ for subjects within S/T groups. So, $df = 12$.

▶ *Students* (i.e., S): There are two levels:

$$df = n - 1 = 2 - 1 = 1.$$

▶ *Teaching Methods* (i.e., T): There are two levels:

$$df = n - 1 = 2 - 1 = 1.$$

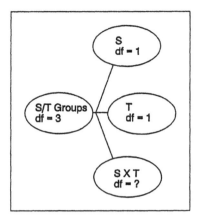

Figure 4.4.   Supplementary variance breakdown for this worked example.

▶ S × T *Interaction*: There are two ways to do this. Therefore, each provides a check for the other, because both methods must give the same answer.

(**i**) We can work out the degrees of freedom by subtraction, as shown in Figure 4.4:

$$df = 3 - 1 - 1 = 1.$$

(**ii**) The degrees of freedom for any interaction are equal to the degrees of freedom for the two parts of the interaction multiplied together. So,

$$\begin{aligned} df &= df\,S \times df\,T \\ &= 1 \times 1 \\ &= 1. \end{aligned}$$

▶ ANOVA SUMMARY TABLE

We have now done all the calculations we need to do using the original scores and the breakdown diagrams. So, we now have all of the

TABLE 4.2   Completed ANOVA Summary Table

Source	SS	df	MS	F	p
Student (S)	144	1	144	108	<0.01
Teaching Method (T)	64	1	64	48	<0.01
S × T Interaction	16	1	16	12	<0.01
Subjects Within S/T Groups	16	12	1.33		
Totals for SS and df	240	15			

information necessary to fill in the first two columns of the ANOVA summary table. The completed summary table is shown in Table 4.2. In the two-factor independent-groups design, there are three points of interest, two main effects and an interaction effect. In our example, we've referred to these as S, T, and S × T. All three of these effects are tested against the Subjects Within S/T Groups, which is therefore the **error term** for all three effects. We'll now show how the three results are obtained.

Calculation of Mean Squares

The mean squares are calculated by dividing each SS by the associated df. Therefore,

$$\text{Student (S) MS} = \frac{144}{1} = 144,$$

$$\text{Teaching Method (T) MS} = \frac{64}{1} = 64,$$

$$\text{S} \times \text{T Interaction MS} = \frac{16}{1} = 16.$$

Calculation of the Error Term in This Design

In this design, the three MS values of interest are each divided by the same error term MS. This is the MS for subjects within S/T groups. Therefore,

$$\text{Error Term MS} = \frac{16}{12}$$

$$= 1.33.$$

Calculation of F Values

To get the F values for the three effects, the three MS values of interest are each divided by the error term MS, that is, 1.33. In each case, the degrees of freedom for the F values are found by using the respective effect's df and the error term's df. Therefore,

$$S: \quad F(1, 12) = 108,$$
$$T: \quad F(1, 12) = 48,$$
$$S \times T \text{ Interaction:} \quad F(1, 12) = 12.$$

p Levels

The last step involves finding the level of statistical significance that each of the F values attained. This is done precisely as in the previous chapter. For each F value, use the df of the numerator and the df of the denominator to check out the 5% critical values table. You will find that all three F values attain statistical significance at the 5% level. This means that you can then check out the 1% critical values table. You will find that three F values also attain statistical significance at the higher 1% level. Therefore,

$$S: \quad F(1, 12) = 108, \qquad p < 0.01,$$
$$T: \quad F(1, 12) = 48, \qquad p < 0.01,$$
$$S \times T \text{ Interaction:} \quad F(1, 12) = 12, \qquad p < 0.01.$$

These results tell us three things:

▶ We have evidence at the 1% level that the levels of the factor Type of Student differ. Therefore, there is a statistically significant difference in the test results between undergraduate students and graduate students.

▶ We have evidence at the 1% level that the levels of the factor Type of Teaching Method differ. Therefore, Method 1 and Method 2 lead to statistically significantly different marks on the test.

▶ We have evidence at the 1% level of an interaction effect, that is, an interaction between the two factors. What does this result mean? It means that *the change in test scores from Method 1 to Method 2 was significantly different for undergraduates than it was for graduates.* This will become clearer when we use the appropriate group means to interpret these results.

Interpreting Our Results

Next, we need to interpret the results in the full context of the experiment. As just noted, the means calculated earlier (see Group Means and the Grand Mean) are very useful. They are as follows:

	Method 1	Method 2	
Undergraduates	9	7	$\overline{X} = 8$
Graduates	17	11	$\overline{X} = 14$
	$\overline{X} = 13$	$\overline{X} = 9$	

Let's use these means to interpret our results.

▶ We have strong evidence (at the $p < 0.01$, or the 1% level) that undergraduates and graduates differed in their performance. The F value told us that there was a statistically significant difference, but it did not tell us which group did better. We need to examine the means to determine this. Looking at the means, we see that, overall, undergraduates averaged 8 marks and graduates averaged 14 marks. So, graduates performed significantly better.

▶ We have strong evidence (at the 1% level) that the teaching methods differed in how effective they were. The F value told us that there was a statistically significant difference, but it did not tell us which method led to better test scores. Looking at the overall means, Method 1 led to a mean overall score of 13, and Method 2 led to a mean overall score of 9. So, Method 1 proved to be significantly more effective.

▶ Now, let's consider the interaction term. We also have strong evidence (at the 1% level) of a significant interaction. To understand this, *we need to look at the treatment means.* Undergraduates scored, on average, 9 marks after Method 1 and 7 marks after Method 2. That is, they did a little better when taught by Method 1. Now consider graduate students. Graduates scored, on average, 17 marks after Method 1 and 11 marks after Method 2. That is, they did much better when taught by Method 1.

In other words, undergraduates did an average of 2 marks better when taught by Method 1, while graduates did an average of 6 marks better. This *relative difference between the two teaching methods for each type of student* is what the interaction effect examines. The significant interaction *F* value told us that the groups did not change in the same way, and looking at the means explained the nature of this difference.

KEY CONCEPTS

Interaction Effects

Two-factor designs allow us to investigate the interaction between two sources of variation, that is, two influences of interest. This can not be done by running two separate experiments that each focuses on one of the influences of interest.

It is important to note here that *the interaction-effect result gives us information over and above the information given by the two main-effect results.* The Type of Student main effect told us that graduates do better than undergraduates overall and the Type of Teaching Method main effect told us that Method 1 is more effective than Method 2 overall. What the interaction effect tells us is that Method 1 has *a significantly greater benefit for graduate students than it does for undergraduates.*

Drawing a graph, as shown in Figure 4.5, can be helpful here in understanding the nature of the interaction effect. Generally, graphs are very useful in representing the results of many statistical analyses. Unless you are particularly good at interpreting a collection of num-

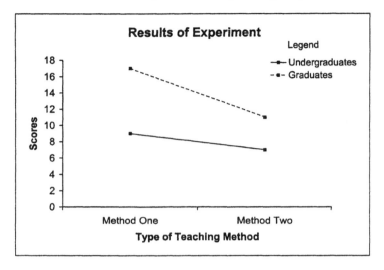

Figure 4.5.   Interaction diagram.

bers, graphs may make the results of an experiment more clear for you. Graphs should have both axes labeled clearly. They should also have a key to all the symbols plotted, as well as a short descriptive title. When a graph is used to show the nature of an interaction effect, the term **interaction diagram** is used.

Graphs provide a visual way of interpreting an interaction effect. In Figure 4.5, we drew lines connecting the means for each pair of treatments. *If, in any interaction diagram, these lines are parallel, there is no interaction.* As soon as the lines depart from being parallel, there is indeed an interaction, but not necessarily a *significant* interaction. In real-life experiments, we know that there are always going to be differences among groups; it is the significance of these differences that is important. Although there can certainly be significant interactions where the lines do not cross, if the lines actually cross there is very likely to be a significant interaction.

A Word of Caution

A word of caution is in order here. When we have a significant interaction, the interpretation of the main effects is no longer simple. That is because the effect of one factor is not the same for all levels of the other factor. In our example, this means that the effect of Teaching Method was different for the two groups of Students. More technically, the significant interaction tells us that there is some variation among the group means that is not accounted for by either of the factors alone. These factors have interacted to produce the pattern of group means that we observed. This was seen in our formula for the interaction SS. There was some variation left over in the S/T groups SS after removing the variance associated with Students and Teaching Methods. Therefore, in our interpretation, we should place more emphasis on the significant interaction than on the significant main effects.

SUMMARY

This chapter discussed two-factor independent-groups design and analysis. As for the one-factor independent-groups ANOVA discussed in the previous chapter, each subject provides only one score. Hence, both ANOVAs fall into the "independent-groups ANOVAs" category. However, in this two-factor design, two sources of variance can be investigated in the same experiment, along with the interaction between these two sources. Often, the interaction effect proves to be of great interest.

⊙———EXERCISES———⊙

1. A group of middle-aged persons were randomly assigned to one of four exercise groups: aerobic training with strength training, aerobic training without strength training, strength training alone, and a no-training control group. Heart rates after 8 weeks of treatment were recorded. Mean heart rates (bpm) for the four groups were 66, 68, 73, and 77, respectively. In addition, the mean heart rate for persons who did aerobic exercise was 67, and was 75 for those who did no aerobic training. The mean heart rate for those who did strength training was 69.5 and for those who did no strength training the mean heart rate was 72.5. The following ANOVA results were obtained:

Main Effect of Aerobic Training (Present vs. Absent): $F(1, 40) = 12.35$, $p < 0.01$,
Main Effect of Strength Training (Present vs. Absent): $F(1, 40) = 2.84$, $p = \text{ns}$,
Interaction of Aerobic and Strength Training: $F(1, 40) = 4.04$, $p = \text{ns}$.

Provide a full interpretation of the results.

2. Male and female students were tested on their knowledge of history by way of either an essay (E) examination or a multiple-choice (MC) examination. Their results are as follows:

Male E	Male MC	Female E	Female MC
72	78	89	71
66	77	81	70
68	69	83	69
70	81	78	73

Perform a two-factor independent-groups ANOVA and provide a full interpretation of the results.

REPEATED-MEASURES ANALYSIS OF VARIANCE

ONE-FACTOR
REPEATED-MEASURES
ANALYSIS OF VARIANCE

Introduction to Part 3

B efore discussing the topic of this chapter, the one-factor repeated-measures ANOVA, it is appropriate to highlight the key difference between the two designs just discussed in Part 2 (independent-groups ANOVAs) and the three designs about to be discussed in Part 3 (repeated-measures ANOVAs).

Difference Between Independent-Groups
ANOVAs and Repeated-Measures ANOVAs

The defining feature of **independent-groups designs** is that *subjects provide one score each*. That is, different groups of subjects (independent groups) provide the scores for each level of each factor.

Chapter 3 looked at the one-factor independent-groups design, and Chapter 4 discussed the two-factor independent-groups ANOVA.

In contrast, subjects in **repeated-measures designs** provide more than one score. We'll look at three of these. In this chapter, we'll focus on the **one-factor repeated-measures ANOVA**. Here, each subject provides a score for each level of the single factor under study. Chapter 6 will then discuss the **two-factor mixed-measures design**, in which subjects provide scores for every level of one factor but not for the other. To understand the concept of this design, consider an experiment in which Age is one factor and 20–30 years of age and 60–70 years of age are the two levels of this factor. The other factor is Reaction Time, and the two levels (tasks) are an auditory task and a visual task. Because a given subject cannot be placed in both age groups, he or she can provide scores for only one level of the Age factor. However, subjects can provide scores for both of the levels of the Reaction Time factor, hence the name "mixed-measures" design. Given that one factor contains repeated measures, this design is discussed in the repeated-measures section (the current section) of this book.

Then, in Chapter 7, we'll discuss a design in which subjects provide scores for all levels of both factors. This is called the **two-factor repeated-measures design**. When it is possible to use this design, it is extremely useful and informative to do so.

Assumptions Underlying Repeated-Measures Designs

In addition to the three assumptions of independence, normality, and homogeneity of variances made for the t test and the F test we discussed in Chapter 3, repeated-measures tests require another assumption to be valid. This assumption is called **sphericity**. One way to think of sphericity is as an extension of the homogeneity of variances assumption. In the repeated-measures case, the **covariances** (the way the scores vary together) among the scores of each level of the repeated-measures factor are assumed to be identical. This assumption needs to be considered when there are more than two repeated measures and in any main effect or interaction involving repeated measures.

In practice, this assumption is almost always violated in the behavioral sciences. The result of this violation is almost always a positive bias such that we "find" a significant difference when one does not really exist. In more technical terms, we reject the **null hypothesis** in cases in which it is, in fact, true. The null hypothesis states that the groups we are investigating do not significantly differ from each other. When we obtain a statistically significant F value (or other significant values in other types of tests), we reject the null hypothesis. When we obtain a nonsignificant result, we do not reject it.

"Finding" a significant difference when one does not really exist is called a **Type I error**. (This is to be distinguished from a **Type II error**, which occurs when we conclude that the null hypothesis is true when it is, in fact, false. That is, we do not find a significant difference that does indeed exist.) Fortunately, a number of solutions to this problem have been suggested.

KEY CONCEPTS

Null Hypothesis

The null hypothesis states that the groups we are investigating do not significantly differ from each other. This hypothesis is then tested by our experiment. When we obtain a statistically significant F value, we reject the null hypothesis. When we obtain a nonsignificant result, we do not reject it.

KEY CONCEPTS

Type I Errors and Type II Errors

A Type I error occurs when we "find" a significant difference that does not really exist. A Type II error occurs when we do not find a significant difference that does indeed exist.

One solution is to analyze the repeated measurements as if they were multiple dependent variables. This approach, based on the multivariate analysis of variance (MANOVA), solves the problem by avoiding the assumption of sphericity altogether. The other type of solution is based on our estimating the degree of violation of the sphericity assumption and correcting our statistical test to compensate for the positive bias. This estimate is called ε.

The MANOVA approach and most approaches based on ε corrections require complicated computations that are beyond the scope of this book. However, one ε-based correction can be calculated easily and we will illustrate its use later. The problem with this correction is that it tends to be very conservative, that is, it tends toward Type II errors. Therefore, the other approaches, which are readily available in most computer packages, are generally to be recommended.

One-Factor Repeated-Measures Analysis of Variance

Now back to the topic of this chapter, the one-factor repeated-measures design. In this design, there is only one factor of interest, but each subject provides a score for every level of this factor. ANOVAs can theoretically handle any number of levels, but, in practice, many informative studies contain two or three levels.

Imagine an experiment in which four people were tested at the end of each week during a 3-week training program. Each person thus provides three scores. The factor "Time of Test—Weeks" is thus a repeated-measures factor, because every subject provides a score in every level (i.e., Week 1, Week 2, and Week 3) of that factor.

Before describing the calculations we use in the repeated-measures ANOVA, it is worth noting here that this analysis is also known as a **two-factor ANOVA with one fixed factor and one random factor**. Looking at the way we present data in this design, shown in Table 5.1, will explain this alternative name. You can see that there is a factor along the left-hand side of the diagram and also along the top of the diagram. However, there is a crucial difference between the factors: *Subjects is a **random factor** and Time of Test—Weeks is a **fixed factor**.*

TABLE 5.1	Experimental Data for the Four Subjects			
		Time of Test—Weeks		
		1	2	3
	S_1	2	5	8
Subjects	S_2	4	4	9
	S_3	5	8	10
	S_4	5	7	9

What do these terms mean? A fixed factor is a factor that would be kept exactly the same if we did the same experiment again. We are interested in how the training course is progressing, and so we test people at three particular times. If we did the experiment again, we would use exactly the same times. That is, we would use *exactly the same levels again.*

On the other hand, a random factor is a factor in which the "levels" were selected randomly from a larger population of levels that could have been chosen. In this experiment, the "levels" are subjects, and each subject is a level. Say four students taking a class in psychology took part in this experiment, but there may have been 100 or more people in the course. That is, those four subjects *were selected at random.* If we did the experiment again, and four subjects were again chosen at random, it is highly likely that a different set of four would be chosen.

In behavioral science experiments, Subjects is by far the most common random factor. Others can occur, but this is rare. Experiments with more than one random factor need to be analyzed by special techniques beyond the scope of this book.

So, Let's Answer the Question on Your Mind . . .

Why does this design have two names; is it a one-factor analysis or a two-factor analysis? Well, strictly, it is a two-factor analysis, but, *for all practical purposes, it is a one-factor analysis.* Strictly, it does involve calculations addressing both the random factor and the fixed factor, but *only one of these factors, the fixed factor, is ultimately of interest to us.* We already know that subjects differ from each other in all sorts of ways. So, as far as the random factor (Subjects) is concerned, this experiment will not tell us anything that we didn't already know. The experiment will, however, provide new information concerning the fixed factor, Time of Test—Weeks. It will tell us whether or not students' performance changes significantly across time.

Having said this, it is important to note here that calculating the variance associated with the random factor is a very useful integral component of this design. Even though we already know that subjects generally differ from each other, *calculating the degree to which they differ from each other in this particular experiment will enable us to investigate the topic of real interest, the fixed factor, more informatively.* This benefit of the design will become clear as we work through this chapter.

Continuing Now With Our Worked Example ...

Having made the preceding points about repeated-measures designs in general and the one-factor repeated-measures ANOVA specifically, let's continue with our worked example. Four subjects took part in a 3-week training program, and an aspect of their performance was assessed by a test at the end of each week. The research question is: Does performance change over the course of the training program?

TABLE 5.2   Experimental Data With Appropriate Totals Also Shown

| | | Time of Test—Weeks | | | |
		1	2	3	Total
Subjects	S_1	2	5	8	15
	S_2	4	4	9	17
	S_3	5	8	10	23
	S_4	5	7	9	21
	Total	16	24	36	76

Table 5.1 presented the scores for the four subjects earlier in the chapter when discussing the layout used for this design. As we've discussed several topics since then, Table 5.2 presents these scores again, along with some totals that will be useful in our calculations.

Group Totals and the Grand Total

The totals of interest are:

$$\text{Week 1} = 16,$$
$$\text{Week 2} = 24,$$
$$\text{Week 3} = 36,$$
$$\text{Grand Total} = 76.$$

In this design, some of the variance that occurs is **between-subjects variance** and some is **within-subjects variance,** because we have more than one subject, and each subject gives more than one score. (This is true *in all repeated-measures analyses.*) Therefore, the first step in the process of splitting up (i.e., partitioning) the variance in repeated-measures designs is always to create two parts, between-subjects variance and within-subjects variance, as shown in Figure 5.1.

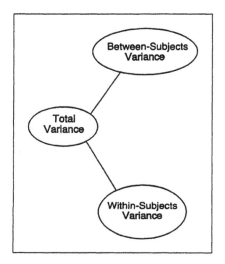

Figure 5.1. Variance breakdown for one-factor repeated-measures ANOVA.

In the course of the analysis, we will use the total score for each subject, even though ultimately we are not interested in the difference between subjects. Therefore, we also need the totals for subjects:

$$\text{Subject 1} = 15,$$
$$\text{Subject 2} = 17,$$
$$\text{Subject 3} = 23,$$
$$\text{Subject 4} = 21.$$

Group Means

The group means of interest are those for Weeks (let's shorten Time of Test—Weeks to just Weeks):

$$\text{Week 1 Mean} = 4,$$
$$\text{Week 2 Mean} = 6,$$
$$\text{Week 3 Mean} = 9.$$

Correction Factor

The correction factor is calculated as usual:

$$
\begin{aligned}
\text{CF} &= \frac{(\sum X)^2}{n} \\
&= \frac{76^2}{12} \\
&= \frac{5776}{12} \\
&= 481.33.
\end{aligned}
$$

Total Sum of Squares

This is calculated as usual:

$$
\begin{aligned}
\text{Total SS} &= \sum X^2 - \text{CF} \\
&= 2^2 + 4^2 + \cdots + 9^2 - \text{CF} \\
&= 550 - 481.33 \\
&= 68.67.
\end{aligned}
$$

Between-Subjects Sum of Squares

This is a measure of the difference between one subject and another, on average. That is, it reflects the difference in subjects' overall performance. The between-subjects SS is calculated by squaring the subject totals, dividing each of these values by the number of scores that made up that total, adding the resulting values together, and subtracting the correction factor. In notation form,

$$\text{Between-Subjects SS} = \frac{15^2}{3} + \frac{17^2}{3} + \frac{23^2}{3} + \frac{21^2}{3} - \text{CF}$$
$$= \frac{225 + 289 + 529 + 441}{3} - \text{CF}$$
$$= 494.66 - 481.33$$
$$= 13.33.$$

Within-Subjects Sums of Squares: Weeks SS and Subjects × Weeks SS

The within-subjects variance reflects to what extent the same subject makes different scores on different occasions. There are two causes of this, shown in Figure 5.2. The top part of Figure 5.2, Weeks (or Time of

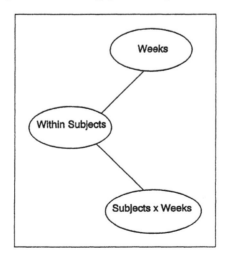

Figure 5.2. Within-subjects variance breakdown.

Test—Weeks), represents the average change in score from each occasion of testing to each other occasion of testing. This is the part we are really interested in, because it represents the Time of Test effect, that is, whether there is a reliable difference between the times. The bottom part represents the idiosyncratic change from week to week exhibited by individual subjects, that is, the fact that individuals do not all show the same change from week to week. (Look at the table and you will see that no two subjects show exactly the same pattern of change across the 3 weeks.) The bottom part of the variance bubble diagram is influenced by both Subjects *and* Weeks, and it is called the **"Subjects by Weeks interaction"** (or the "Subjects times Weeks interaction"), denoted "Subjects × Weeks." The word *interaction* shows that these two influences, Subjects and Weeks, are interacting to give us this part of the overall variance, called the Subjects × Weeks sum of squares.

Having partitioned the within-subjects variance as shown in Figure 5.2, we now calculate the Weeks SS. This is done by squaring the week totals, dividing each of these values by the number of scores that

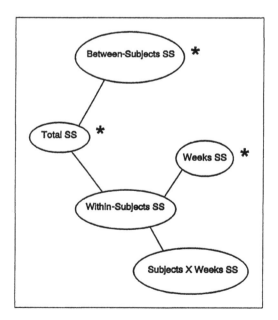

Figure 5.3. Calculation of Subjects × Weeks SS.

made up that total, adding the resulting values together, and subtracting the correction factor:

$$\text{Weeks SS} = \frac{16^2}{4} + \frac{24^2}{4} + \frac{36^2}{4} - \text{CF}$$
$$= 532 - 481.33$$
$$= 50.66.$$

Having calculated the Weeks SS, we can calculate the Subjects × Weeks SS by using Figure 5.3 and doing some subtraction. Again, the asterisks represent the bits that can be calculated easily. So, by subtraction,

$$\text{Within-Subjects SS} = \text{Total SS} - \text{Between-Subjects SS}$$
$$= 68.67 - 13.33$$
$$= 55.33,$$
$$\text{Subjects} \times \text{Weeks SS} = \text{Within-Subjects SS} - \text{Weeks SS}$$
$$= 55.33 - 50.66$$
$$= 4.67.$$

ANOVA SUMMARY TABLE ◀

We can now put these values into the ANOVA summary table for this design (see Table 5.3). The table used here is different from those used in Part 2 because the nature of the analysis is different.

TABLE 5.3   ANOVA Summary Table for This Design

Source	SS	df	MS	F	p
Between-Subjects	13.33				
Within-Subjects					
Weeks	50.66				
Subjects × Weeks	4.67				

Degrees of Freedom

We now need to calculate the degrees of freedom associated with each SS. We can use the same diagram (Figure 5.3) to help us. Each time a part was "asterisked" because the SS could be calculated easily, the same holds true for the df.

▶ *Total*: We started with 12 scores:

$$df = n - 1$$
$$= 12 - 1$$
$$= 11.$$

▶ *Between Subjects*: There were four subjects:

$$df = n - 1$$
$$= 4 - 1$$
$$= 3.$$

▶ *Within Subjects*: By subtraction,

$$df = \text{Total df} - \text{Between-Subjects df}$$
$$= 11 - 3$$
$$= 8.$$

(There is another way to think of this. We are dealing within subjects here. Let's work out the df within each subject. There are three scores, and thus $3 - 1 = 2$ df. There are four subjects altogether, so the total number of dfs for "Within subjects" is $4 \times 2 = 8$.)

▶ *Weeks*: There are 3 weeks:

$$df = n - 1$$
$$= 3 - 1$$
$$= 2.$$

► *Subjects × Weeks*: By subtraction,

$$df = \text{Within-Subjects df} - \text{Weeks df}$$
$$= 8 - 2$$
$$= 6.$$

(*There is another way to think of the df for any interaction: The df for an interaction is the product of the individual dfs. Think of the × symbol as a multiplication sign just for this purpose, as an aid to memory here:*

$$\text{Subjects × Weeks df} = \text{Subjects df × Weeks df}$$
$$= \text{Between-Subjects df × Weeks df}$$
$$= 3 × 2 = 6.)$$

Completed ANOVA Table

We can now construct the full ANOVA summary table, shown in Table 5.4.

There are several points to note here:

► The mean squares are again calculated by dividing the SS by the appropriate df.

► In general, we do not calculate F values for random factors. Therefore, no F value appears for Subjects (or, technically, for "between subjects").

TABLE 5.4   Completed ANOVA Summary Table

Source	SS	df	MS	F	p
Between-Subjects	13.33	3	—		
Within-Subjects					
Weeks	50.66	2	25.33	32.47	<0.01
Subjects × Weeks	4.67	6	0.78		

▶ The F value of interest is that for Weeks. To get this F value, the MS for Weeks is compared with (divided by) the MS for the "Subjects × Weeks" interaction. That is,

$$F = \frac{\text{MS Weeks}}{\text{MS Subjects} \times \text{Weeks}}.$$

For all F values, the item of interest is compared with our best estimate of the variance that occurs by chance alone. In other words, if there is a real effect, the variance caused by the item of interest will be significantly greater than the variance owing to chance. So, our estimate of chance variance (the error term) always goes on the bottom (i.e., is the denominator) of the F-value calculation. Put another way:

$$F = \frac{\text{Variance of Interest}}{\text{Variance of Noninterest}}.$$

In this particular analysis, the MS for "Subjects × Weeks" is used as the error term for Weeks. Therefore,

$$F = \frac{25.33}{0.78}$$
$$= 32.47.$$

The full result is, therefore,

$$F(2,6) = 32.47, \qquad p < 0.01.$$

However, you will recall from our discussion earlier in this chapter that this result is based on the assumption of sphericity. Because this assumption is almost always violated in the behavioral sciences, a correction is called for. We stated earlier that a correction called ε has been suggested to estimate the degree of violation of the sphericity assumption. This estimate ranges from 1, which indicates sphericity and thus no violation, to $1/(k-1)$ (where k is the number of repeated measurements), which indicates the maximum violation of sphericity.

To apply this correction, we simply multiply the numerator and denominator degrees of freedom by ε and look up our F value with these new degrees of freedom to come up with our p value. Most estimates of ε are beyond the scope of this book but one suggested by Geisser and Greenhouse in 1958 is easy to calculate. This approach assumes maximum violation of sphericity and thus ε equals $1/(k-1)$. In practice, we simply divide the numerator and denominator degrees of freedom by the degrees of freedom associated with the repeated measures factor, that is, $(k-1)$.

In the present case, we have three repeated measurements, so we divide the numerator and denominator degrees of freedom by $3-1$, that is, 2. This gives us our final answer:

$$F(1,3) = 32.47, \qquad p < 0.05.$$

Interpretation

We have statistical evidence (at the 5% level) that the Time of Test—Weeks did affect the scores. We now need to look at the means to complete our interpretation. These were:

Week 1   4
Week 2   6
Week 3   9

Thus, the performance of the participants in the program increased significantly across the weeks of the course.

Multiple Comparisons

While the preceding statement is a true one, that interpretation can actually be taken another step. As we saw in Chapter 3, when a factor has more than two levels, it is possible to get a significant F, but to find that only some of the levels differ significantly from each other. In that chapter, we saw that specific statistical tests can be applied to test whether the difference between each and every pair of levels attains statistical significance. On that occasion, an appropriate multiple-comparison strategy involved the independent-groups t test. We'll now show you how another form of the t test can be used in the context of the present chapter, that is, in the context of repeated-measures designs.

A multiple-comparison strategy that is appropriate here is the use of the **dependent-measures t test**. The dependent-measures t test, sometimes called the t test for related measures, compares two sets of scores *from the same group of subjects* and allows us to determine whether the means of the sets of scores differ significantly. Because the sets of scores to be compared come from the same subjects, there will be the same number of scores in each group.

Dependent-Measures t Test

First, we'll present an example using two sets of scores, A and B. Then we'll return to the current worked example concerning performance across weeks of the course.

Ten subjects provided scores on two occasions. They actually performed a memory test following the administration of Drug A and Drug B. The two sets of scores, A and B, are measures of performance on the memory test. In this example, there are 10 subjects. So, $N = 10$. The research question is: Is performance on the memory test different following administration of Drug A from performance following administration of Drug B? The data are:

Subject	Drug A	Drug B
1	7	9
2	4	6
3	3	7
4	8	5
5	3	6
6	2	6
7	5	2
8	1	2
9	0	3
10	3	4

The calculations to be performed are as follows:

1. Calculate the difference between each pair of scores (a pair being the two scores for a given subject). When doing this, we must perform the subtractions in the same manner for each pair of scores. We'll (arbitrarily) choose to subtract the score for Drug B from the score for Drug A. Then, add up the difference scores. The sign of each score *must be taken into account in this step*.

Subject	Drug A	Drug B	Difference $(D) = A - B$
1	7	9	−2
2	4	6	−2
3	3	7	−4
4	8	5	3
5	3	6	−3
6	2	6	−4
7	5	2	3
8	1	2	−1
9	0	3	−3
10	3	4	−1

$$\sum D = 6 + (-20)$$
$$= 6 - 20$$
$$= -14.$$

2. Calculate the average difference, $\overline{D}$:

$$\overline{D} = \frac{-14}{10}$$
$$= -1.4.$$

3. Calculate $\sum D^2$:

$$\sum D^2 = (-2)^2 + \cdots + (-1)^2$$
$$= 78.$$

4. Calculate $(\sum D)^2$:

$$\left(\sum D\right)^2 = (-14)^2$$
$$= 196.$$

5. Calculate $\sum D^2 - (\sum D)^2 / N$:

$$\sum D^2 - \frac{(\sum D)^2}{N} = 78 - \frac{196}{10}$$
$$= 78 - 19.6$$
$$= 58.4.$$

Now, we substitute these calculated values into the following equation:

$$t = \frac{\overline{D}}{\sqrt{\dfrac{\sum D^2 - \dfrac{(\sum D)^2}{N}}{N(N-1)}}}$$

$$= \frac{-1.4}{\sqrt{\dfrac{58.4}{90}}}$$

$$= -1.74.$$

Degrees of Freedom

To check the significance of the t-test result, we need to know the associated degrees of freedom. For this t test, these are the total number of subjects minus 1. That is,

$$df = N - 1.$$

This expression of the degrees of freedom appears in the basic equation for calculating the t value (see formula above).

In our example,

$$df = 10 - 1$$
$$= 9.$$

Therefore,

$$t(9) = -1.74.$$

At this point, we can ignore the minus sign in front of our t value (we'll cover this thoroughly in a moment) and simply use the result "$t(9) = 1.74$." To determine the significance of this result, we first check the 5% table. Our result does not attain significance at the 5% level. So, we can stop at this point, because we know that the result cannot attain significance at the 1% level. Therefore,

$$t(9) = 1.74, \qquad \text{ns.}$$

Interpreting this result, the two sets of scores do not differ significantly. Therefore, there is no statistical evidence that Drug A and Drug B influence performance on the memory test differently.

A Calculation Note: When to Take Account of Minus Signs

As mentioned previously, at this final stage we can ignore the minus sign in front of the t value. However, in contrast, it was vital *not to ignore the positive and negative signs when calculating the algebraic sum of the difference scores in Step 1 of the calculations.* (The difference scores without a minus sign in front of them have a positive sign by default, even though this is not usually written. This convention is true for all positive numbers, whatever the context.)

Why can we ignore the negative sign at the end, and yet have to take the negative signs into account earlier in Step 1? The answer to this question comes in two parts. First, we must take into account the negative signs in Step 1 because *all subtractions of one of the scores in a pair from the other must be done in the same direction.* This is simply the way that this t test works. That is, we must subtract all the A scores from the B scores, or, alternatively, all the B scores from the A scores. It does not matter which way round we do this, but we must be consistent. In Step 1, we stated that we would arbitrarily choose to subtract the score for Drug B from the score for Drug A. This choice led directly to the difference scores obtained.

We could, however, equally well have decided to subtract the score for Drug A from the score for Drug B in every case. This would have resulted in a different set of difference scores. What would the precise nature of this difference have been? If you go back and do the calculations again, you will see that the numbers (the absolute values) are the same in each case, *but the sign in front of each difference score is opposite to the sign in the former case.* This means that the mean difference score is now +1.4, written simply as 1.4.

The second part of our answer is that, while the sign in front of the mean difference score changes, *every other part of the calculation comes out to be exactly the same.* The reason for this is that, for the other two calculations involving difference scores, the necessary step of squaring certain items makes the difference between a positive sign and a negative sign disappear. (Recall from our discussion of the calculation of the sums of squares in Chapter 2 that a negative number multiplied by another negative number, in this case by itself, gives a positive answer.) So, $\sum D^2$ and $(\sum D)^2$ turn out to be identical. This, in turn, means that the sign in front of the t value depends purely on the arbitrary choice of subtracting A from B or subtracting B from A. Therefore, we can ignore the sign in front of the t value when checking the level of significance obtained.

Back to this Chapter's Worked Example

In this chapter's worked example, you'll remember that we have three sets of scores, Week 1, Week 2, and Week 3. To find out how these sets differ significantly, we can perform three comparisons using three dependent-measures t tests:

1. Compare Week 1 and Week 2.

2. Compare Week 2 and Week 3.

3. Compare Week 1 and Week 3.

If you work through the three *t* tests following the method described previously, you will see that the results for these comparisons are as follows:

Comparison 1: $t(3) = 2.83$, ns,

Comparison 2: $t(3) = 4.24$, $p < 0.05$,

Comparison 3: $t(3) = 12.25$, $p < 0.01$.

Now that we have the mathematical answers from the multiple comparisons, we need to interpret them in the context of our experiment. We'll also use the group means that we've already calculated. Our interpretation is as follows:

1. There is no statistical evidence that performance at Week 2 was significantly better than at Week 1.

2. There is evidence at the 5% level that performance at Week 3 was better than performance at Week 2.

3. There is evidence at the 1% level that performance at Week 3 was better than performance at Week 1.

As in Chapter 3, we deliberately used three levels in this worked example to demonstrate how multiple comparisons (this time employing the dependent-measures *t* test) are conducted. You'll recall that multiple comparisons are not needed when there are only two levels. If a significant *F* value is obtained in a one-factor ANOVA when there are only two levels, then there is only one possible interpretation: *The two levels differ significantly from each other*, and the group means tell you which group's scores are larger (i.e., they tell you the direction of the significant difference).

KEY CONCEPTS

Dependent-Measures *t* Test

This test is useful for conducting multiple comparisons when the factor of interest has more than two levels.

An Interesting Question Concerning One-Factor Repeated-Measures ANOVAs and Dependent-Measures *t* Tests

At this point, just as in Chapter 3, you may be asking yourself a very reasonable question: Since we needed *t* tests after our one-factor ANOVA to get a complete answer to our research question, could we simply have conducted the three *t* tests in the first place instead of performing the ANOVA? That is, in this case, can the dependent-measures *t* test strategy be used in place of the one-factor repeated-measures ANOVA design?

The answer, as in Chapter 3, is yes. Indeed, if one knows in advance what comparisons are of interest, the multiple-comparison approach using *t* tests may be more appropriate. However, the argument presented in Chapter 3 in support of ANOVAs is again true here. That is, there is a definite two-part advantage in studying the one-factor ANOVA design when more than two levels are present. First, if one does not have any prior ideas about which comparisons are of interest, the one-factor repeated-measures ANOVA design provides a very efficient way to test for differences among sets of scores generated by the same subjects. Second, an understanding of the one-factor repeated-measures ANOVA design is a big help in understanding the two-factor ANOVA designs involving repeated measures that are discussed in the next two chapters.

The Power of an ANOVA

At this point, we'll discuss the **power** of a particular ANOVA. The power of an analysis is its ability to find a difference when there really is a difference present. Expressed in more technical terms, it is its ability to reject the null hypothesis when it should be rejected.

The one-factor repeated-measures ANOVA is a more powerful design than the one-factor independent-groups ANOVA. *It is almost always more powerful to compare experimental conditions as a within-subjects effect than to compare them as a between-subjects effect.* In other words, it is almost always better if each subject does each of the conditions, as is the case in the repeated-measures design.

To illustrate this point, let's take a set of scores from an experiment designed to investigate the effect of time of visual exposure to objects on later recall of the objects. A tray containing 20 items is presented to a subject for 10 seconds, 20 seconds, or 30 seconds; the task then is to write down as many items as possible. In Experiment A, there were 12 subjects, and each subject did only one condition (four subjects did each). In Experiment B, there were only four subjects, who each did all three conditions. The results are shown in Tables 5.5 and 5.6.

You can carry out a full analysis of variance on both sets of data. The two ANOVA summary tables are shown in Tables 5.7 and 5.8. As you can see, the two different analyses give very different results, *even*

TABLE 5.5 Data from Experiment A, Which Used a One-Factor Independent-Groups Design

	Time (seconds)	
10	20	30
11	12	13
8	10	12
5	8	11
4	6	8

though the data (scores) used are identical. The null hypothesis in both cases would have been "Time spent looking at the objects does not affect ability to recall the objects." Experiment A did not provide evidence to reject the null hypothesis. In contrast, Experiment B provided strong evidence (at the 1% level of significance) to reject the null hypothesis.

Why do the different analyses produce different results? The answer to this question is a very illuminating one. The total SS will be exactly the same in each case because we are analyzing exactly the same scores. Additionally, therefore, the total variance will be identical in each case.

TABLE 5.6   Data from Experiment B, Which Used a One-Factor Repeated-Measures Design

	Time (seconds)		
	10	20	30
S_1	11	12	13
S_2	8	10	12
S_3	5	8	11
S_4	4	6	8

TABLE 5.7   Completed ANOVA Summary Table for Experiment A

Source	SS	df	MS	F	p
Time Lengths	32	2	16	2.25	ns
Subjects Within Time Lengths	64	9	7.1		

TABLE 5.8   Completed ANOVA Summary Table for Experiment B

Source	SS	df	MS	F	p
Between-Subjects	60	3	—	—	—
Within-Subjects					
Time Lengths	32	2	16	24	<0.01
Subjects × Time Lengths	4	6	0.67		

However, *the way in which the variance is partitioned differs between the two analyses.*

This definition of the *F* test is applicable to all ANOVAs:

$$F = \frac{\text{Variance of Interest}}{\text{Variance of Noninterest}}.$$

In every case, we want to use our best estimate of both variances in this formula. Consider first the variance of interest, namely, that attributable to Time. Look at Tables 5.7 and 5.8 and you will see that the SS, df, and MS for Time are identical in both cases. That is, *our best estimate of the variance of interest is identical in both ANOVAs.* However, look at the tables again and you will see that *the error term against which our effect of interest is tested differs considerably.* The error term is always our best estimate of the variance of noninterest, and therefore *our best estimate of the variance of noninterest differs considerably.*

In the independent-groups design, all the variance that is not attributable to Time is attributable to Subjects Within Time, the error term for that design. Therefore, the MS of the effect of interest (16) is divided by 7.1, giving an *F* value of 2.25. This value did not attain statistical significance. In the repeated-measures design, however, the variance not attributable to Weeks was split up in two ways, into Between Subjects and Time × Subjects. The error term in this design, Time × Subjects, therefore, ends up being much smaller than in the independent-groups design. Here, the error term MS was 0.67, and the MS of the effect of interest (16) divided by 0.67 gives an *F* value of 24. This value obtained significance at the 1% level.

KEY CONCEPTS

The Power of an ANOVA

The power of an analysis is its ability to reject the null hypothesis when it should be rejected or, put the other way round, its ability to find a difference that does indeed exist.

SUMMARY

In this chapter, we introduced the one-factor repeated-measures ANOVA. We explained when it is appropriate to use this design and showed how to perform all the necessary steps required by the analysis.

We also considered the topic of the power of an ANOVA. The power of an analysis is its ability to find a difference when there really is a difference present, that is, its ability to reject the null hypothesis when it should be rejected. When it is possible to employ a repeated-measures design to investigate a research question, it is a good idea to do so because a repeated-measures design will almost always be more powerful than an independent-groups design.

The topic of multiple comparisons was discussed again. This time, the test of interest was the dependent-measures t test. The dependent-measures t test is useful in conjunction with a repeated-measures design when the factor of interest has more than two levels.

EXERCISES

1. A group of pilots were tested on their reaction times to a visual target presented on a screen after a full night's sleep and after being sleep deprived for 30 hours. Their mean reaction times were 869 milliseconds after a full night's sleep and 1236 milliseconds after being sleep deprived. The ANOVA results were

$$F(1, 14) = 46.3, \qquad p < 0.01.$$

Provide a full interpretation of the results.

2. A group of six athletes were tested on their performance on a novel task before and after training. The number of errors they committed are as follows:

Time 1	Time 2
9	6
10	8
11	8
13	9
8	7
8	5

Perform a one-factor repeated-measures ANOVA and provide a full interpretation of the results.

TWO-FACTOR
MIXED-MEASURES
ANALYSIS OF VARIANCE

In this chapter, we'll discuss the two-factor mixed-measures ANOVA. The layout for this design is presented in Table 6.1, using six subjects in this example. Unlike the one-factor repeated-measures design, in which the subjects could not be divided into groups and each subject was regarded as a level, the six subjects here are broken into two clearly defined groups. Each group is a level of Factor A. Now consider Factor B. Each of the subjects provides a score for every level of Factor B. In this example, Factor B has three levels, and so each subject provides three scores.

In the two-factor mixed-measures design, then, one factor (Factor A in Table 6.1) contains independent groups while the other factor (Factor B in Table 6.1) contains repeated measures. This leads directly to the words "mixed measures" in the name of this design. Factor A is

TABLE 6.1   Layout for Two-Factor Mixed-Measures ANOVA

			Factor B		
			Level 1	Level 2	Level 3
Factor A	Group 1 (Level 1)	S_1			
		S_2			
		S_3			
	Group 2 (Level 2)	S_4			
		S_5			
		S_6			

often referred to as the **"between-subjects" variable**, and Factor B as the **"within-subjects" variable**.

Breakdown Diagram for This Design

Let's start by considering the breakdown diagram for this design, shown in Figure 6.1. The first thing to note is that there is variance both between subjects and within subjects. We have different groups (independent groups) of subjects contributing between-subjects variance. We also have several scores per subject contributing within-subjects variance. So, the first part of the breakdown is very easy.

KEY CONCEPTS

Two-Factor Mixed-Measures Design

In this design, one factor contains independent groups (the "between-subjects" variable) while the other factor contains repeated measures (the "within-subjects" variable), hence the name "mixed-measures" design.

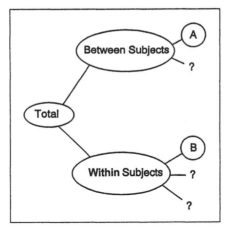

Figure 6.1. Variance breakdown for two-factor mixed-measures ANOVA.

Because Factor A is a between-subjects factor, that part of the variance breakdown will come out of the between-subjects bubble in the diagram. Conversely, because Factor B is a within-subjects factor, that part will come out of the within-subjects bubble. Then, there are three more sources of variation that we need to consider. One comes out of the top bubble and the other two come out of the bottom bubble. These three sources are shown as question marks in Figure 6.1.

1. *Subjects Within Factor A Groups.* In our example, there are two groups. Within each group, subjects will differ a bit from each other. So, within each group, we get some within-groups variance. When we add up the variances within each group, we get the **subjects within Factor A groups variance.** This component of the breakdown forms the error term against which Factor A is tested.

Think of this test in these terms. If the difference between the mean of Group 1 and the mean of Group 2 is large and the variance within each group is small, we'll very probably get a significant difference. However, if the variance within each group is large, we may not.

2. *Factor A × Factor B Interaction.* This is the variance due to the interaction of the two factors. This comes out of the within-subjects bubble.

3. *Factor B × Subjects Within Factor A Groups Interaction.* The **Factor B × subjects within Factor A groups interaction** term also comes out of the within-subjects bubble. It forms the error term for both Factor B and the Factor A × Factor B interaction.

Think of it this way. "Subjects within Factor A groups" describes the way in which subjects' scores averaged across all levels of Factor B differ between subjects in Group 1 and subjects in Group 2. What the interaction of this term with Factor B measures is the way that, within these averages, subjects will differ in what they scored on each particular level of Factor B. For example, consider two subjects who happen to score a total of 30 on the three levels of Factor B. This means that they each have an average of 10. Within these averages, however, one subject may have scored 9, 10, and 11, and another 14, 10, and 6. So, although the averages are the same, there is still variation. The Factor B × Subjects within Factor A Groups interaction term captures this variance.

Worked Example

Now let's look at a worked example, which will help us to think in terms of real factors, rather than talking about Factor A and Factor B.

We are going to do an experiment to examine the effects of a drug, Drug X, on cognitive performance over a period of time. Four subjects will receive Drug X, and four subjects will receive a placebo (no subject actually knows which was received). Each subject will be tested three times: at 10 minutes, 20 minutes, and 30 minutes after drug administration. The test will be a test of cognitive performance. The scores obtained will be the time taken to complete a task, measured in seconds. The research question is: Does Drug X affect performance?

Before we start, you may wonder why we need the second group of subjects. Why not just test the subjects who are given Drug X? If that strategy were adopted, we could not be sure that any effects observed were due to the drug. It could be argued that they were simply due to the passing of time and the fact that people get tired by the time of the third test (if performance declines across time), or the fact that people become better at the task due to practice (if performance increases across time). The second group (the **placebo control group**) of subjects therefore provides results that will enable us address these issues at the end of the study.

KEY CONCEPTS

Control Groups

Control groups are extremely useful in some designs. For example, they can tell us what we would expect if a group of subjects did a test several times in the absence of the main experimental manipulation. These control subjects might get better, perform about the same, or get worse. The results of the group receiving the manipulation of interest can then be judged against those of the controls.

The eight subjects are randomly assigned to either the Drug X group or the placebo control group by the experimenter. Subjects therefore do not know which group they are in (they may not know how many groups there are in the study). The subjects are therefore **blind** to their group status. (In large-scale studies of this nature, such as clinical trials conducted by pharmaceutical and biotechnology companies, the experimenters administering the test may not know which group subjects are in. This information is coded, and the code is known only by people who reveal it *after* the experiment has been completed and the results analyzed. This type of study is called a **double-blind** design.)

The factors in our worked example are:

Factor A: Drug Type   Levels: Drug X, Placebo
Factor B: Time of Test   Levels: 10 min, 20 min, 30 min

Drug Type contains two independent groups (subjects are either in one group or the other), and Time of Test contains repeated measures (every

TABLE 6.2   Experimental Data to Be Analyzed

| | | \multicolumn{4}{c}{Factor B—Times} |
| | | \multicolumn{4}{c}{Time of Test (min)} |

		10	20	30	Total
Factor A—Drugs / Drug X	S_1	28	25	34	
	S_2	23	30	32	
	S_3	25	30	35	
	S_4	24	35	39	360
Placebo	S_5	28	22	24	
	S_6	24	23	22	
	S_7	23	26	21	
	S_8	21	21	21	276
	Total	196	212	228	636

subject provides a score at each of these times, i.e., at each of the levels of this factor). The results are shown in Table 6.2.

The first steps in the analysis have already been taken. Totals for each level of each factor and the grand total have been calculated. Before actually starting the computations, it is a good idea to obtain other totals that we shall need at various points in the analysis. We shall need treatment totals, that is, totals for the groups formed by each pair of levels. The treatments are: Drug X and 10 min, Drug X and 20 min, Drug X and 30 min, Placebo and 10 min, Placebo and 20 min, and Placebo and 30 min. These treatments, or Drugs/Times groups, can be seen easily in the layout. Let's draw a set of boxes, which corresponds exactly to the layout of the results:

Time of Test

Drug X	100	120	140
Placebo	96	92	88

Each number in these boxes is the total of the four scores that appear in the corresponding box in Table 6.2.

We shall also need subject totals, that is, the total of each subject's three scores. For Subject 1, this total is $(28 + 25 + 34)$, which is 87. The

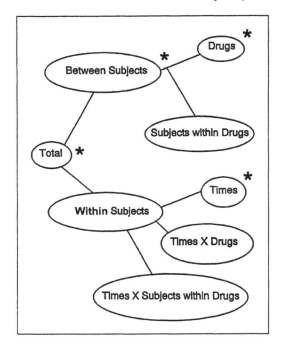

Figure 6.2. Variance breakdown for this worked example.

totals for the eight subjects are: 87, 85, 90, 98, 74, 69, 70, and 63, respectively.

The bubble diagram for this analysis is shown in Figure 6.2, and the calculations for this ANOVA are as follows:

Group Totals and the Grand Total

We've already calculated these. The values are shown in Table 6.2.

Group Means

These can be calculated by dividing the group totals by the number of scores making up each total, i.e., dividing by 4:

Drug X, 10 min: 25   Placebo, 10 min: 24
Drug X, 20 min: 30   Placebo, 20 min: 23
Drug X, 30 min: 35   Placebo, 30 min: 22

Correction Factor

This is calculated as usual using the formula

$$CF = \frac{(\sum X)^2}{n}$$

$$= \frac{636^2}{24}$$

$$= 16854.$$

Total Sum of Squares

This is calculated as usual using the formula

$$\text{Total SS} = \sum X^2 - CF$$

$$= 17492 - 16854$$

$$= 638.$$

Between-Subjects Sum of Squares

This is calculated using the formula

$$\text{Between-Subjects SS} = \frac{87^2}{3} + \frac{85^2}{3} + \cdots + \frac{63^2}{3} - CF$$

$$= 17201.33 - 16854$$

$$= 347.33.$$

(*Why divide by 3? Because three scores made up each total.*)

Drugs Sum of Squares

This is calculated using the formula

$$\text{Drugs SS} = \frac{360^2}{12} + \frac{276^2}{12} - CF$$

$$= 17148 - 16854$$

$$= 294.$$

(*Why divide by* 12? *Because there are* 12 *scores altogether in each level of Drugs. We ignore the other factor temporarily.*)

Subjects Within Drugs Sum of Squares

We use subtraction to get this SS. From the breakdown diagram,

Between-Subjects SS = Drugs SS + Subjects Within Drugs SS.

Therefore,

$$\begin{aligned} \text{Subjects Within Drugs SS} &= \text{Between-Subjects SS} - \text{Drugs SS} \\ &= 347.33 - 294 \\ &= 53.33. \end{aligned}$$

So far, we've calculated the top part of the bubble diagram, that is, the between-subjects bubble and the two parts of the variance that come out of that bubble. Now we can start on the bottom part of the bubble diagram.

Within-Subjects Sum of Squares

We use subtraction to get this term. From the breakdown diagram,

Total SS = Between-Subjects SS + Within-Subjects SS.

Therefore,

$$\begin{aligned} \text{Within-Subjects SS} &= \text{Total SS} - \text{Between-Subjects SS} \\ &= 638 - 347.33 \\ &= 290.67. \end{aligned}$$

Times Sum of Squares

Here, we are dealing with one of the two main effects. So, we temporarily ignore the other (Drugs) and find the totals for each level of this factor. As we saw in Table 6.2, these are 196, 212, and 228. These are squared and divided by the number of scores that made up each total. We then add these values and subtract the CF:

$$\text{Times SS} = \frac{196^2}{8} + \frac{212^2}{8} + \frac{228^2}{8} - \text{CF}$$
$$= 16918 - 16854$$
$$= 64.$$

Times × Drugs Interaction Sum of Squares

To calculate this term, we need a subsidiary breakdown diagram. This diagram, which is shown in Figure 6.3, is used only for the purposes of this particular calculation. Three of the four bubbles in this breakdown have asterisks by them. This means that we can calculate them easily. In fact, we've already calculated two of them, Times and Drugs. We now calculate the Times/Drugs SS, and we can then obtain what we want, namely, the Times × Drugs interaction SS, by subtraction.

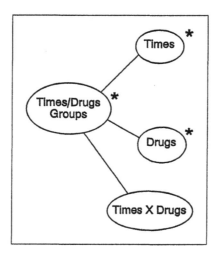

Figure 6.3. Subsidiary variance breakdown for this worked example.

As we noted earlier in this worked example, Times/Drugs groups are the groups (treatments) made by combining one level of one factor with one level of the other factor. These treatments are seen as the six "boxes" in the initial layout of results. We need the totals, and we calculated them (100, 120, 140, 96, 92, and 88) earlier.

To get the Times/Drugs Groups SS, we square these, divide by four, add up these values, and subtract the CF:

$$\text{Times/Drugs Groups SS} = \frac{100^2}{4} + \frac{120^2}{4} + \cdots + \frac{88^2}{4} - \text{CF}$$
$$= 17356 - 16854$$
$$= 502.$$

We can now obtain the term we want, the Times × Drugs SS, by subtraction. From the new subsidiary breakdown, we know that

Times/Drugs Groups SS = Times SS + Drugs SS + Times × Drugs SS.

Therefore,

$$\text{Times} \times \text{Drugs SS} = \text{Times/Drugs Groups SS} - \text{Times SS} - \text{Drugs SS}$$
$$= 502 - 64 - 294$$
$$= 144.$$

Having obtained the term we wanted, we now forget all about the subsidiary breakdown diagram and deal only with the main one.

Times × Subjects Within Drugs Sum of Squares

This term is found by subtraction. From the main breakdown diagram,

Within-Subjects SS = Times SS + Times × Drugs SS
+ Times × Subjects Within Drugs SS.

Therefore,

$$\text{Times} \times \text{Subjects Within Drugs SS} = \text{Within-Subjects SS} - \text{Times SS}$$
$$- \text{Times} \times \text{Drugs SS}$$
$$= 290.67 - 64 - 144$$
$$= 82.67.$$

▶ ANOVA SUMMARY TABLE

We now simply put all these values into the first column (SS) of the appropriate ANOVA summary table. The ANOVA summary table for this example is shown in Table 6.3. Next, we'll see how to complete the summary table.

Degrees of Freedom

The calculation of the degrees of freedom for this design is as follows:

▶ *Total*: We have 24 scores:

$$\text{df} = n - 1$$
$$= 24 - 1$$
$$= 23.$$

TABLE 6.3   Completed ANOVA Summary Table for This Example

Source	SS	df	MS	F	p
Between-Subjects					
Drugs	294	1	294	33.07	<0.01
Subjects Within Drugs	53.33	6	8.89		
Within-Subjects					
Times	64	2	32	4.64	<0.05
Times × Drugs	144	2	72	10.45	<0.01
Times × Subjects Within Drugs	82.67	12	6.89		
Total	638	23			

► *Between Subjects*: Following the breakdown diagram (just as the SS values add up throughout the diagram, so too do the df values), let's look at between subjects next. We have eight subjects:

$$\text{df} = n - 1$$
$$= 8 - 1$$
$$= 7.$$

► *Within Subjects*: From the breakdown diagram, we can get this value by subtraction:

$$\text{Total} = \text{Between Subjects} + \text{Within Subjects}.$$

Therefore,

$$\text{Within Subjects} = \text{Total} - \text{Between Subjects}$$
$$= 23 - 7$$
$$= 16.$$

(There is another way to think of this. We want the df for within subjects. So, let's look at each subject. Each subject provides three scores to give the total for that person. So, within each subject, there are $3 - 1 = 2$ df. We have eight subjects. So, the within-subjects df $= 2 \times 8 = 16$.)

► *Drugs*: The factor Drugs has two levels. Thus,

$$\text{df} = n - 1$$
$$= 2 - 1$$
$$= 1.$$

► *Subjects Within Drugs*: From the breakdown diagram, we can get the df here by subtraction:

$$\text{Between Subjects} = \text{Drugs} + \text{Subjects Within Drugs}.$$

Therefore,

$$\text{Subjects Within Drugs} = \text{Between Subjects} - \text{Drugs}$$
$$= 7 - 1$$
$$= 6.$$

(There is another way to think of this. What we are calculating is the df value for "subjects within Drug groups." In each Drug group (Drug X and placebo), there are four subjects. So, in each Drug group, there are $4 - 1 = 3$ df. We have two groups. So, altogether, there are $2 \times 3 = 6$ df.)

▶ *Times*: The factor Times has three levels. Therefore,

$$\text{df} = n - 1$$
$$= 3 - 1$$
$$= 2.$$

▶ *Times* × *Drugs Interaction*: The df for an interaction is the product of the df of each part of the interaction term. Therefore,

$$\text{df} = \text{df for Times} \times \text{df for Drugs}$$
$$= 2 \times 1$$
$$= 2.$$

▶ *Times* × *Subjects Within Drugs*: Again, the df for this interaction term can be found by multiplying together the df for each part of the interaction term. Therefore,

$$\text{df} = \text{df for Times} \times \text{df for Subjects Within Drugs}$$
$$= 2 \times 6$$
$$= 12.$$

So, we now have all the df values we need for the ANOVA summary table. This table can now be completed. The mean squares, MS, are calculated as before by dividing each sum of squares, SS, by the respective degrees of freedom. The three F values are then calculated for the three effects, Drugs, Times, and Times × Drugs interaction, by dividing the MS for each effect by the appropriate error term MS. We have already discussed this point for this design.

The degrees of freedom for each F value are the dfs of the respective MSs that were used in their calculation. So, we have

1. *Drugs*:

$$F(1,6) = 33.07, \qquad p < 0.01.$$

2. *Times*:

$$F(2,12) = 4.64, \qquad p < 0.05.$$

3. *Times × Drugs Interaction*:

$$F(2,12) = 10.45, \qquad p < 0.01.$$

Interpretation of Results

1. *Drugs*: We have evidence that the type of drug administered does indeed differentially affect cognitive performance. We have evidence for this at the 1% ($p < 0.01$) level of significance.

2. *Times*: We have evidence at the 5% level of significance ($p < 0.05$) that the length of time elapsed since the administration of the drugs affects cognitive performance.

3. *Times × Drugs Interaction*: We have evidence (at the 1% level of significance) of an interaction; that is, there is a significant interaction between the type of drug administered and the length of time elapsed before testing cognitive performance.

These interpretations are correct, but they do not provide all the information that we need to answer our questions. To do this, we need to

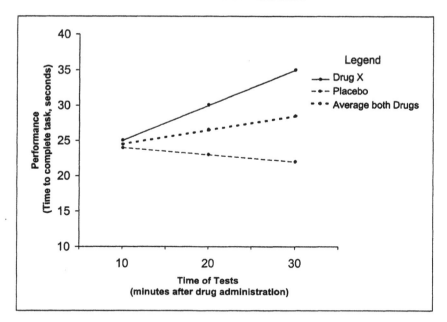

Figure 6.4.   Results of experiment investigating the effects of Drug X on cognitive performance.

look at the treatment means. We can draw a grid and put the means in each appropriate box. It is also a good idea to draw a graph (an interaction diagram—see Figure 6.4) using these means:

	10 min	20 min	30 min
Drug X	25	30	35
Placebo	24	23	22

Using this information, we can interpret the results more fully. Let's consider our three conclusions (one for each F value) again:

1. The type of drug administered does significantly and differentially affect performance. Drug X, on average, resulted in subjects taking $(25 + 30 + 35)/3 = 30$ seconds to complete the test of performance, while the placebo, on average, resulted in subjects taking $(24 + 23 + 22)/3 = 23$ seconds to complete it.

(Just as we ignored "Times" temporarily while doing the calculations for the Drugs SS, our conclusion here does not deal with Times directly. The drug effects are averaged across the level of Times in this part of the analysis.)

2. As the time to testing increased, performance, on average, declined (i.e., performance scores, time in seconds to complete the task, increased). This effect can be seen on the graph as the middle line, which links the performance scores averaged across all subjects for each occasion of testing.

(Just as we ignored "Drugs" temporarily while doing the calculations for the Times SS, our conclusion here does not deal with Drugs directly. The two types of drugs are averaged in this part of the analysis.)

3. It is the fuller interpretation of the interaction effect that is most interesting and illuminating in this example. The interaction diagram shows that while subjects who received the placebo actually improved very slightly across the occasions of testing, those who received Drug X became worse across the occasions of testing. So, we can also make some observations about Drug X from these data. Looking at the results for 10 minutes after drug administration, Drug X subjects and subjects receiving the placebo were about the same in performance. So, Drug X doesn't seem to be acting yet. After 20 minutes, however, it is making performance decline (i.e., subjects are taking longer to complete the task), and after 30 minutes it is making performance still worse.

The deduction that it is actually Drug X that is having this effect, as opposed to performance becoming worse simply because subjects had become tired by doing the tasks already, is helped by the evidence from the subjects who received the placebo instead of Drug X. They, on average, actually became slightly better (i.e., took less time) across the occasions of testing. These results again emphasize the fact that the interpretation of the main effects is not a simple task when a significant interaction is obtained, and they highlight the tremendous value of control groups in some studies. We need to do a lot of thinking before we do our experiments, so that we design (and conduct) them in such a way that we will be able to answer our research question.

One Last Point Here: Consider Drug Z

Just before leaving the two-factor mixed-measures design, consider Drug Z. Pretend that we did the same experiment again, only we used Drug Z this time. Another eight subjects were chosen. The results are shown in Table 6.4.

If we did the analysis again, *the ANOVA summary table would be identical*. By comparing this set of data with the previous set in Table 6.2, you will see that the values for 20 minutes and 30 minutes have simply been interchanged. (If we had *really* done another experiment, we know that the chances of getting precisely the same scores are incredibly small; the same scores are used here simply to make a point.) Because the scores used in the analysis are identical, the three F values are identical. However, *our interpretation of the pharmacological effects on cognitive performance will change considerably.*

TABLE 6.4   Results Using Drug Z

| | | Time of Test | | |
		10	20	30
Drug Z	S_1	28	34	25
	S_2	23	32	30
	S_3	25	35	30
	S_4	24	39	35
Placebo	S_5	28	24	22
	S_6	24	22	23
	S_7	23	21	26
	S_8	21	21	21

This difference in interpretation can be seen very clearly by drawing the interaction diagram for this new analysis. The means we need are the same as before, but in a different order:

	10 min	20 min	30 min
Drug Z	25	35	30
Placebo	24	22	23

The last two columns have, in effect, simply been changed around. The effect of this alteration on the interaction diagram is shown in Figure 6.5.

Drug Z certainly affects cognitive performance, *but its biggest effect is seen 20 minutes after administration.* By 30 minutes, performance seems to be returning to the level of the control group. So, Drug Z seems to have different pharmacological properties from Drug X.

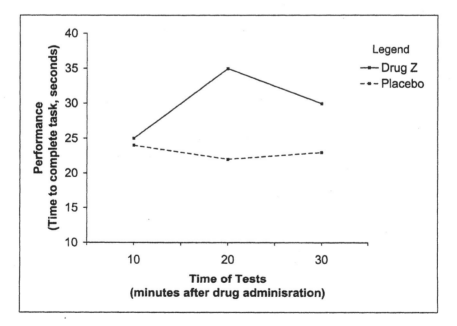

Figure 6.5. Results of experiment investigating the effects of Drug Z on cognitive performance.

This potentially very important difference, however, could not have been seen simply by looking at the F values. A full interpretation was necessary to see the nature of the difference. The graphic representation of the experimental results (the interaction diagram) was a very useful illustration of the difference.

This point is made to emphasize once again the fact that the numerical results of an ANOVA, or indeed any statistical test, are not enough. We must interpret the results in the context of the experiment we conducted.

SUMMARY

In this chapter, we have examined the two-factor mixed-measures design. Unlike the one-factor repeated-measures design, in which the subjects could not be divided into groups and each subject was regarded as a level, subjects in this design can be broken into two or more clearly defined groups. Each group of subjects is a level of the "between-subjects" factor. Each subject in the experiment provides a score for every level of the other factor, the "within-subjects" (i.e., the repeated-measures) factor.

This design is useful when two factors are of interest, but subjects cannot complete more than one level of one of the factors. If age is of interest in a two-factor design, and the levels are "less than 30 years of age" and "over 60 years of age," a given subject cannot fit into both age groups. That is, the age factor cannot contain repeated measures. On the other hand, a second factor (such as the ability to perform a certain task early in the morning and later in the day) could indeed contain repeated measures. This design is therefore a widely used one.

⊙——— EXERCISES ———⊙

1. A group of patients with depression and a group of nonde-
    pressed persons were asked to remember a happy event and
    a sad event. The mean of their scores on a measure of nega-
    tive mood were as follows:

Depressed group, happy memory	5
Depressed group, sad memory	8
Nondepressed group, happy memory	3
Nondepressed group, sad memory	5

    The mean across all memories for the depressed group was
    6.5 and the mean across all memories for the nondepressed
    group was 4.0. In addition, the mean for the happy mem-
    ory across groups was 4.0 and the mean for the sad memory
    across groups was 6.5. The ANOVA results were as follows:

    Main effect of Group (depressed vs. nondepressed):

    $$F(1,28) = 3.56, \qquad p = \text{ns.}$$

    Main effect of Memory (happy vs. sad):

    $$F(1,28) = 2.99, \qquad p = \text{ns.}$$

    Interaction of Group and Memory:

    $$F(1,28) = 4.00, \qquad p = \text{ns.}$$

    Provide a full interpretation of these results.

2. A group of high school students and a group of college stu-
    dents performed a mirror tracing task on two occasions. The
    number of errors they committed are as follows:

High School		College	
Time 1	Time 2	Time 1	Time 2
13	10	6	4
15	10	8	4
17	9	6	2
17	7	9	3
14	8	10	3

Perform a two-factor mixed-measures ANOVA and provide a full interpretation of the results.

TWO-FACTOR
REPEATED-MEASURES
ANALYSIS OF VARIANCE

In our earlier discussions of one-factor ANOVAs, we noted that, when possible, it is almost always more powerful to test an effect as a within-subjects effect than as a between-subjects effect. Exactly the same logic applies to two-factor ANOVAs. The design discussed in this chapter, the two-factor repeated-measures design, is therefore a particularly powerful one.

In this design, each subject provides a score for every level of both factors. That is, every subject receives every treatment. This contrasts to the design discussed in the previous chapter (the two-factor mixed-measures ANOVA), in which one factor contained repeated measures while the other factor contained independent groups.

This design therefore tests both factors as within-subjects effects. Because of the way this analysis is performed (think back to the one-factor repeated-measures design discussed in Chapter 5), we get a sum of squares for subjects that can be "removed" from the analysis. We know that subjects will differ from each other, and so analysis of this influence is not of interest to us. Partitioning the variance accordingly allows us to remove the subject SS and focus on the effects of interest.

It is true that it is not always possible to use this design. Imagine that age is one of the factors of interest in a two-factor design, and that "less than 30 years of age" and "over 60 years of age" are the two levels. (The other factor contains levels that are all done by both age groups.) One subject cannot fit into both age groups. That is, the age factor cannot contain repeated measures. In a case such as this, the two-factor mixed-measures design discussed in the previous chapter could be used successfully. However, whenever it is possible to use the two-factor repeated-measures ANOVA design, it is a good idea to do so.

Layouts for This Design

There are two common ways of setting out the data from a two-factor repeated-measures design, both of which turn out to be helpful in obtaining the different totals that we need to perform the necessary calculations. First, we'll look at the layout that is more similar to those we've already seen. We'll consider the simplest example of this design, where each of the two factors A and B have only two levels.

Consider an experiment that involves six subjects. We'll put Factor A along the side of the layout, and Factor B along the top. The layout is shown in Table 7.1. There are six scores in each treatment box, but the same six subjects provide the scores in each and every treatment.

The second layout is less similar to those we've seen earlier, but it has the advantage that it visually emphasizes that each subject gives a score in all combinations of levels, that is, all treatments. All the data from a given subject appear in one row, making it easy to look at that subject's performance across all treatments. This layout is shown in Table 7.2. Because the second layout makes it easy to scan across a row and see all the data from a given subject, it is preferred by some other textbooks, and it may be the only one they present. However, as noted previously,

TABLE 7.1   First Possible Layout for the Two-Factor Repeated-Measures ANOVA Design

		Factor B	
		Level 1	*Level 2*
Factor A — Level 1	S_1		
	S_2		
	S_3		
	S_4		
	S_5		
	S_6		
Level 2	S_1		
	S_2		
	S_3		
	S_4		
	S_5		
	S_6		

TABLE 7.2   Second Possible Layout for the Two-Factor Repeated-Measures ANOVA Design

	A_1		A_2	
	B_1	B_2	B_1	B_2
S_1				
S_2				
S_3				
S_4				
S_5				
S_6				

A_1 and A_2 are the two levels of Factor A, and B_1 and B_2 are the two levels of Factor B.

we'll use both layouts because each one helps us to calculate necessary totals.

The sources of variance that appear in the two-factor repeated-measures design are shown in Table 7.3, the ANOVA summary table (we'll discuss how the degrees of freedom and mean squares are obtained in more detail in a while). In this chapter, we will not use bubble diagrams, because that approach becomes rather complex for this design. Instead, we'll use the formulas given in Table 7.3.

TABLE 7.3   ANOVA Summary Table for This Design

Source	SS	df	MS	F	p
Between-Subjects		$n-1$			
Within-Subjects		$npq - n$			
Factor A		$p-1$			
Factor B		$q-1$			
Factor A × Factor B		$(p-1)(q-1)$			
Subjects Within A		$(p-1)(n-1)$			
Subjects Within B		$(q-1)(n-1)$			
Subjects Within A × B		$(p-1)(q-1)(n-1)$			
Total		$npq - 1$			

Similarities and Differences Between This Design and Previous Two-Factor Designs

This design has some similarities and some differences when compared to the previous designs we've studied. First, we'll highlight the similarities. As for all two-factor ANOVAs (the independent-groups design, the mixed-measures design, and the present repeated-measures design), there are three results of interest. An F value is calculated for Factor A, for Factor B, and for the interaction between these main effects. Then, as we constantly emphasize, these F values must be interpreted. This interpretation is done in the same manner as in previous chapters.

Now we'll consider how this design differs from previous cases. In this design, there are three error terms. Each effect of interest (Factor A, Factor B, and the interaction between them) is tested against a different error term. The arrows in Table 7.3 show which error term is used in each instance (we'll cover this in the text also). Table 7.3 also shows how the df values are calculated. The letter n represents the number of subjects, p represents the number of levels in Factor A, and q represents the number of levels in Factor B. This means that some of the calculations in this analysis are performed differently than those we've seen earlier. However, the general principles behind the calculations are the same.

Worked Example

Our example in this chapter concerns subjects' ability to hear certain sounds when background noise is present. In this experiment, six subjects have to sit in a room and listen carefully, pushing a button in front of them each time they hear a short, sharp tone (the stimulus). Pushing the button shows that the subject detected the stimulus. On this occasion, speed of response (reaction time) is not of interest. We simply want to know whether, for each stimulus, subjects are able to detect the stimulus or not.

The subjects will do two sessions of listening. In one session, there will be background noise made up of low-frequency sounds and in the other there will be background noise made up of high-frequency sounds. Two stimuli will be used in the experiment: a low-frequency stimulus and a high-frequency stimulus. During the two sessions (low-frequency background noise, high-frequency background noise), subjects will be presented with a total of 30 low-frequency stimuli and a total of 30 high-frequency stimuli. The score for each subject in each treatment will be the number of times he or she detects the stimulus. The research question is: Do background noises affect ability to detect different stimuli?

Before we go through the calculations, you might want to pause and think about methodology, that is, all the necessary experimental controls you would have to use in actually conducting an experiment like this. You could discuss these with your classmates. Some of the issues you'd be concerned with would include: presenting stimuli in counterbalanced order, the relative amplitudes of the background noises to each other and to the amplitudes of the stimuli, and the relative amplitudes of the stimuli.

Our factors, then, are:

Factor A: Background Noise	Two Levels:
	Low Frequency and High Frequency
Factor B: Stimulus	Two Levels:
	Low Frequency and High Frequency

TABLE 7.4   Experimental Data to Be Analyzed (First Layout)

			Factor B—Stimulus		
			Low Frequency	High Frequency	Total
Factor A—Background Noise	Low Frequency	S_1	12	18	
		S_2	9	20	
		S_3	9	22	
		S_4	10	22	
		S_5	9	17	
		S_6	11	23	182
	High Frequency	S_1	20	8	
		S_2	24	10	
		S_3	16	9	
		S_4	18	11	
		S_5	18	10	
		S_6	22	12	178
	Total		178	182	360

Both factors contain repeated measures, and so every subject provides a score for every treatment. The results are shown in the first of our two possible layouts in Table 7.4. The first steps in the analysis, calculating the grand total and the totals for each level of each factor, have been done and the results are shown in Table 7.4. The grand total is 360 and the totals for each level of each factor are:

Low-Frequency Background Noise   182
High-Frequency Background Noise   178 } Levels of Background Noise
Low-Frequency Stimulus   178
High-Frequency Stimulus   182 } Levels of Stimulus

At this time, it is a good idea to calculate some other totals that we shall need at various points in this analysis. Retabulating the data into the second layout helps here. This retabulation and some more useful totals are shown in Table 7.5. This layout gives us the treatment totals, that is, totals for the groups formed by each pair of levels.

TABLE 7.5 Experimental Data to Be Analyzed (Second Layout)

	Background Noise				
	Low Frequency		*High Frequency*		
	Low-Frequency Stimulus	*High-Frequency Stimulus*	*Low-Frequency Stimulus*	*High-Frequency Stimulus*	*Total*
S_1	12	18	20	8	58
S_2	9	20	24	10	63
S_3	9	22	16	9	56
S_4	10	22	18	11	61
S_5	9	17	18	10	54
S_6	11	23	22	12	68
Total	60	122	118	60	360

Thus:

Total for Low-Frequency Background Noise, Low-Frequency Stimulus = 60,
Total for Low-Frequency Background Noise, High-Frequency Stimulus = 122,
Total for High-Frequency Background Noise, Low-Frequency Stimulus = 118,
Total for High-Frequency Background Noise, High-Frequency Stimulus = 60.

It also gives us the totals for each individual subject across all treatments (58, 63, 56, 61, 54, and 68 for subjects 1–6, respectively).

Calculations

The calculations needed are as follows:

Group Totals and the Grand Total

These have already been calculated.

Group Means and the Grand Mean

Low-Frequency Background Noise/Low-Frequency Stimulus Group = 10,
Low-Frequency Background Noise/High-Frequency Stimulus Group = 20.3,
High-Frequency Background Noise/Low-Frequency Stimulus Group = 19.6,
High-Frequency Background Noise/High-Frequency Stimulus Group = 10,
Grand Mean = 360/24 = 15.

Correction Factor

The correction factor is calculated as usual:

$$CF = \frac{(\sum X)^2}{n}$$

$$= \frac{360^2}{24}$$

$$= 5400.$$

Total Sum of Squares

The total SS is calculated as usual:

$$Total\ SS = \sum X^2 - CF$$

$$= 12^2 + \cdots + 12^2 - CF$$

$$= 6092 - 5400$$

$$= 692.$$

Between-Subjects Sum of Squares

$$Between\text{-}Subjects\ SS = \frac{58^2}{4} + \cdots + \frac{68^2}{4} - CF$$

$$= 5432.5 - 5400$$

$$= 32.5.$$

(*Why did we divide by 4? Because four scores made up each total.*)

Background Noise Sum of Squares

$$Background\ Noise\ SS = \frac{182^2}{12} + \frac{178^2}{12} - CF$$

$$= 5400.66 - 5400$$

$$= 0.66.$$

(*To calculate the Background Noise SS, we temporarily ignore the other factor, Stimulus, and look at the two levels of Background Noise. The totals 182 and 178 are shown in Table 7.4. Why divide by 12? Because 12 scores made up each total.)*

Stimulus Sum of Squares

$$\text{Stimulus SS} = \frac{178^2}{12} + \frac{182^2}{12} - \text{CF}$$
$$= 5400.66 - 5400$$
$$= 0.66.$$

(To calculate the Stimulus SS, we temporarily ignore the other factor and look at the two levels of Stimulus. The totals 178 and 182 are shown in Table 7.4. Why divide by 12? Just like the previous case, the totals are made up of 12 scores each.)

It should be noted here that, in this example, the Background Noise SS and the Stimulus SS turn out to be identical. This will not always be the case. In real experiments, it is extremely unlikely that this would occur. The reason it occurs here is that, as you may well have realized already, we have chosen scores that can easily be plugged into the formulas we use to calculate the necessary values throughout the analysis.

Background Noise × Stimulus Interaction Sum of Squares

To calculate this interaction SS, we use the four totals from each possible combination of levels. These totals were shown in Table 7.5.

Background Noise × Stimulus Interaction SS
$$= \frac{60^2}{6} + \frac{122^2}{6} + \frac{118^2}{6} + \frac{60^2}{6} - \text{CF}$$
$$- \text{Background Noise SS} - \text{Stimulus SS}$$
$$= 6001.34 - 5400 - 0.66 - 0.66$$
$$= 600.02.$$

(Why divide by 6? Because six scores went into each total.)

It is worth noting that due to the rounding errors whereby 2480.66666 etc. and 2320.66666 etc. are rounded up to 2480.67 and 2320.67 here, and 2760.33 and 2640.33 remain as they are in the Background Noise SS calculation, we end up with the answer 600.02 here. If we had used fractions instead of decimals, this number would have been 600 even. So, let's call it 600 from here on.

Subjects Within Background Noise Sum of Squares

This value is the error term for the Background Noise main effect. To calculate this value, we first need to calculate some new totals. We can do this by laying out the data exactly as they appeared in Table 7.4 and then calculating totals for each subject across each level of Background Noise. For example, Subject 1's total for the low-frequency level is $12 + 18 = 30$, and Subject 1's total for the other level, high frequency, is $20 + 8 = 28$. The data and the appropriate totals are shown in Table 7.6.

For each subject for each level of Background Noise, therefore, the total comes from adding two scores, one from each of the two levels of the factor we are currently not interested in (i.e., Stimulus). By adding the two numbers, we are **collapsing across** Stimulus.

TABLE 7.6   Calculating the Subjects Within Background Noise SS

		Scores From Two Levels of Stimulus		Total
Background Noise — Low Frequency	S_1	12	18	30
	S_2	9	20	29
	S_3	9	22	31
	S_4	10	22	32
	S_5	9	17	26
	S_6	11	23	34
High Frequency	S_1	20	8	28
	S_2	24	10	34
	S_3	16	9	25
	S_4	18	11	29
	S_5	18	10	28
	S_6	22	12	34

Note that $12 + 18 = 18 + 12 = 30$. Therefore, for present purposes, it does not matter which score came from which level of Stimulus.

The calculation is as follows:

Subjects Within Background Noise SS

$$= \frac{30^2}{2} + \frac{29^2}{2} + \cdots + \frac{34^2}{2} - \text{CF}$$

$$- \text{Between-Subjects SS} - \text{Background Noise SS}$$

$$= 5452 - 5400 - 32.5 - 0.66$$

$$= 18.84.$$

(*Why divide by* 2? *Because each of the* 12 *totals are made up of two numbers.*)

Subjects Within Stimulus Sum of Squares

This value is the error term for the Stimulus main effect. To calculate this value, we first need to calculate another set of new totals. The easiest way to do this is to retabulate the data. The new table is going to look similar in structure to Table 7.6, but this time we are going to put the factor Stimulus down the side of the table and then calculate the appropriate totals. The retabulated data and these new totals are shown in Table 7.7.

For each subject for each level of Stimulus, the total comes from adding two scores, one from each of the two levels of the factor that we are currently not focusing upon (i.e., Background Noise). By adding the two scores, we are collapsing across Background Noise. Note that $12 + 20 = 20 + 12 = 32$. Therefore, for present purposes, it doesn't matter which score came from which level of Background Noise.

The calculation is as follows:

Subjects Within Stimulus SS

$$= \frac{32^2}{2} + \frac{33^2}{2} + \cdots + \frac{35^2}{2} - \text{CF}$$

$$- \text{Between-Subjects SS} - \text{Stimulus SS}$$

$$= 5460 - 5400 - 32.5 - 0.66$$

$$= 26.84.$$

TABLE 7.7   Calculating the Subjects Within Stimulus SS

			Scores From Two Levels of Background Noise		Total
Stimulus	Low Frequency	S_1	12	20	32
		S_2	9	24	33
		S_3	9	16	25
		S_4	10	18	28
		S_5	9	18	27
		S_6	11	22	33
	High Frequency	S_1	18	8	26
		S_2	20	10	30
		S_3	22	9	31
		S_4	22	11	33
		S_5	17	10	27
		S_6	23	12	35

(*Why divide by 2? Because, once again, the 12 totals were each made up of two numbers.*)

Subjects Within Background Noise × Stimulus Interaction

This is the error term for the Background Noise × Stimulus interaction effect. This term is calculated by subtraction as follows:

Subjects Within Background Noise × Stimulus Interaction SS

= Total SS − Between-Subjects SS

− Background Noise SS − Stimulus SS

− Subjects Within Background Noise SS

− Subjects Within Stimulus SS

− Background Noise × Stimulus Interaction SS

= 692 − 32.5 − 0.66 − 0.66 − 18.84 − 26.84 − 600

= 12.5.

TABLE 7.8 Partially Completed ANOVA Summary Table

Source	SS	df	MS	F	p
Between-Subjects	32.5				
Within-Subjects	659.5				
Background Noise	0.66				
Stimulus	0.66				
Background Noise × Stimulus	600				
Subjects Within Background Noise	18.84				
Subjects Within Stimulus	26.84				
Subjects Within Background Noise × Stimulus	12.5				
Total	692				

We have now completed all of the sum of squares calculations we need for the calculation of our three F values. However, we usually calculate one more. In order to find the total within-subjects SS, we subtract the between-subjects SS from the total SS. Neither the total within-subjects SS nor the between-subjects SS is used to calculate an F value. The total within-subjects SS is broken down into individual informative steps, and we already know that subjects differ from each other. However, the values are usually put in the ANOVA summary table for the sake of completeness in the Source of Variance column. So, let's fill in this part of the ANOVA summary table. This is shown in Table 7.8.

Calculating the Degrees of Freedom

For this design, we'll explain how the degrees of freedom are obtained in a different manner from that employed in previous chapters. Because we didn't use a bubble diagram, we'll go through the sums of squares in the ANOVA summary table in turn and explain how each degree of freedom is calculated.

▶ *Between Subjects*: There are six subjects:

$$\text{df} = n - 1$$
$$= 6 - 1$$
$$= 5.$$

▶ *Total*: We have 24 scores:

$$\begin{aligned} \mathrm{df} &= n - 1 \\ &= 24 - 1 \\ &= 23. \end{aligned}$$

[*There is another way to think of this, as shown by the formula in Table 7.3. The total df is given by* $(npq - 1)$, *where n is the number of subjects, p is the number of levels of Factor A, and q is the number of levels of Factor B. So,* $6 \times 2 \times 2 = 24$, *and* $24 - 1 = 23$. *This formula works because, in this design, every subject provides a score for every level of every factor.*]

▶ *Within Subjects*: This value is obtained by subtraction:

$$\begin{aligned} \text{Within Subjects} &= \text{Total} - \text{Between Subjects} \\ &= 23 - 5 \\ &= 18. \end{aligned}$$

[*There are two other ways to think of this. One is to consider that each subject provides four scores to give the total for that person. So, within each subject, there are* $4 - 1 = 3$ *df. We have six subjects. So, the within-subjects df* $= 3 \times 6 = 18$. *The second is to use the formula given in Table 7.3. That is, within-subjects df* $= (npq - n)$. $npq = 6 \times 2 \times 2 = 24$. $24 - n = 24 - 6 = 18$.]

▶ *Background Noise*: This factor has two levels:

$$\begin{aligned} \mathrm{df} &= n - 1 \\ &= 2 - 1 \\ &= 1. \end{aligned}$$

▶ *Stimulus*: This factor also has two levels:

$$\begin{aligned} \mathrm{df} &= n - 1 \\ &= 2 - 1 \\ &= 1. \end{aligned}$$

▶ *Background Noise × Stimulus Interaction*: The df for an interaction is the product of each part of the interaction term. Thus,

$$df = df \text{ for Background Noise} \times df \text{ for Stimulus}$$
$$= 1 \times 1$$
$$= 1.$$

▶ *Subjects Within Background Noise*: Using the formula in Table 7.3,

$$df = (p-1)(n-1)$$
$$= (2-1)(6-1)$$
$$= 1 \times 5$$
$$= 5.$$

▶ *Subjects Within Stimulus*: Using the formula in Table 7.3,

$$df = (q-1)(n-1)$$
$$= (2-1)(6-1)$$
$$= 1 \times 5$$
$$= 5.$$

▶ *Subjects Within Background Noise × Stimulus Interaction*: Using the formula in Table 7.3,

$$df = (p-1)(q-1)(n-1)$$
$$= 1 \times 1 \times 5$$
$$= 5.$$

We now have all the df values we need for the complete ANOVA summary table. These df values, along with all the other values seen in the completed table, are presented in Table 7.9.

As usual, the MS values are calculated by dividing each SS value by the respective degrees of freedom. The three F values are then calculated for Background Noise, Stimulus, and the Background Noise × Stimulus interaction by dividing the MS for each effect by the

TABLE 7.9   Completed ANOVA Summary Table

Source	SS	df	MS	F	p
Between-Subjects	32.5	5			
Within-Subjects	659.5	18			
Background Noise	0.66	1	0.66	0.18	ns
Stimulus	0.66	1	0.66	0.12	ns
Background Noise × Stimulus	600	1	600	240	$p < 0.01$
Subjects Within Background Noise	18.84	5	3.77		
Subjects Within Stimulus	26.84	5	5.37		
Subjects Within Background Noise × Stimulus	12.5	5	2.5		
Total	692[*]	23[**]			

[*]$692 = 32.5 + 659.5$

[**]$23 = 5 + 18$

appropriate error term MS. Table 7.3 showed us which error term MS is used in each case.

Thus,

1. F Value for Background Noise

$$= \frac{\text{Background Noise MS}}{\text{Subjects Within Background Noise MS}}$$

$$= \frac{0.66}{3.77}$$

$$= 0.18.$$

2. F Value for Stimulus $= \dfrac{\text{Stimulus MS}}{\text{Subjects Within Stimulus MS}}$

$$= \frac{0.66}{5.37}$$

$$= 0.12.$$

3. F Value for Background Noise × Stimulus Interaction

$$= \frac{\text{Background Noise} \times \text{Stimulus MS}}{\text{Subjects Within Background Noise} \times \text{Stimulus MS}}$$

$$= \frac{600}{2.5}$$

$$= 240.$$

The degrees of freedom for each F value are the dfs of the respective mean squares that were used in their calculation. So, we have:

1. Background Noise:

$$F(1,5) = 0.18, \qquad \text{ns.}$$

2. Stimulus:

$$F(1,5) = 0.12, \qquad \text{ns.}$$

3. Background Noise × Stimulus Interaction:

$$F(1,5) = 240, \qquad p < 0.01.$$

Interpretation of Results

Having obtained our three F values and their respective p values, we now need to interpret these results:

1. *Background Noise*: Overall, we do not have evidence that the type of background noise (low frequency or high frequency) significantly affects the ability to detect a stimulus. The F value did not reach statistical significance.

2. *Stimulus*: Overall, we do not have evidence that the type of stimulus (low frequency or high frequency) significantly affects the ability to detect the stimulus. The F value did not reach statistical significance.

3. *Background Noise × Stimulus Interaction*: We have strong evidence (at the 1% level) of a significant interaction. That is, there is a statistically significant interaction between the type of background noise and the type of stimulus in determining the ability to detect the stimulus.

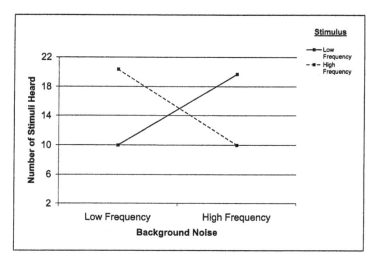

Figure 7.1. Interaction diagram.

To interpret the significant interaction effect more fully, we need to examine the treatment means. First, we can create a grid for the treatment means and put each of the means in the appropriate box:

		Stimulus	
		Low	High
Background	Low	10	20.33
Noise	High	19.67	10

Second, we can draw a graph using these means. This graph, the interaction diagram, is shown in Figure 7.1.

Now, we can give a more thorough interpretation. Let's consider our three effects again:

1. *Background Noise*: The type of background noise does not significantly affect the ability to detect a stimulus. Low-frequency background noise resulted in subjects detecting, on average, $(10 + 20.33)/2 = 15.16$ stimuli. High-frequency background noise resulted in subjects detecting, on average, $(19.67 + 10)/2 = 14.84$ stimuli.

(*Our conclusion here does not deal with Stimuli directly. The Background Noise effects are averaged across the levels of Stimulus.*)

2. *Stimulus*: The type of stimulus does not significantly affect the ability to detect a stimulus. Low-frequency stimuli were detected, on average, $(10 + 19.67)/2 = 14.84$ times. High-frequency stimuli were detected, on average, $(20.33 + 10)/2 = 15.16$ times.
(*Our conclusion here does not deal with Background Noise directly. The Stimuli effects are averaged across the levels of Background Noise.*)

3. *Background Noise × Stimulus Interaction*: Just as in the example in the previous chapter, it is the more complete interpretation of the interaction effect that is the most informative aspect of this experiment. The analysis of the two main effects, Background Noise and Stimulus, showed us that, on average, subjects heard stimuli just as well against both kinds of background noise, and that, on average, subjects heard both types of stimuli equally well. Not only were the differences not statistically significant, but the means were also very close in each case. However, we did obtain a significant result for the interaction effect, and the interaction diagram shows the nature of this interaction very clearly. Consider first the low-frequency stimulus. This was poorly detected against a background of low-frequency noise, but detected much better against a background of high-frequency noise. Now look at the high-frequency stimulus. It was poorly detected against a background of high-frequency noise, but detected much better against a background of low-frequency noise. Our conclusion is that *it is the interaction between the type of background noise and the type of stimulus we are trying to hear that determines how successfully we can hear the stimuli.*

Significant Interactions in the Absence of Significant Main Effects

The conclusions reached from this study may not surprise you. It may also not surprise you to learn that we deliberately chose the scores used in this example to show that it is possible to have a highly significant (and very meaningful) interaction effect even though both main effects were nonsignificant. The interaction diagram shown in Figure 7.1 represents a "textbook" example (please excuse the pun) of this occurrence. The four treatment means create a crossover in the diagram that is almost perfectly symmetrical. The dotted line that represents the low-frequency stimulus goes up from 10 to 19.67, and the solid line representing the high-frequency stimulus goes down from 20.33 to 10. While a real-life experiment of this kind would almost certainly not yield data as symmetrical as those used in this example, the basic shape of the interaction diagram would be similar.

SUMMARY

The two-factor repeated-measures design is a very powerful one, and, when it can be used, we would encourage researchers to do so.

In this design, each subject provides a score for every level of both factors. That is, every subject receives every treatment. Therefore, the design tests both factors as within-subjects effects. Because of the way this analysis is performed, we get a sum of squares for subjects that can be "removed" from the analysis. Because we already know that subjects differ from each other in many ways, analysis of this influence is not of interest to us. Partitioning the variance accordingly allows us to remove the subject sum of squares and focus on the two effects of interest by using repeated-measures on both factors. (We saw the reasons why this approach is a powerful one in Chapter 5.)

We have seen throughout the text that obtaining the best estimate of the variance of noninterest (i.e., the error term against which to test the variance of interest) is a critical part of every ANOVA discussed. The same is true here. In this case, three different error terms are calculated, one for each effect (Factor A, Factor B, and the A × B interaction).

⊙———EXERCISES———⊙

1. It is important for future space travel to know the effects of gravity (or the lack thereof) on muscle strength. A group of astronauts performed a strength test twice on the Earth and then twice while orbiting the Earth. Their scores on Earth were 85 and 83 whereas in orbit the scores were 63 and 60. The average of the scores on Earth was 84 and the average in orbit was 61.5. The average of the scores on the first test (regardless of location) was 74 and the average of the scores on the second test (regardless of location) was 71.5. The ANOVA results were as follows:

    Main effect of Location (Earth vs. space):

    $$F(1,6) = 15.05, \qquad p < 0.01.$$

    Main effect of Repetition (first vs. second):

    $$F(1,6) = 4.97, \qquad p = \text{ns}.$$

    Interaction of Location and Repetition:

    $$F(1,6) = 2.58, \qquad p = \text{ns}.$$

    Provide a full interpretation of the results.

2. A group of patients with an anxiety disorder were presented lists of nonthreat and threat words while either relaxed or after performing a brief bout of exercise on a bicycle. Afterward, they were asked to recall as many words as they could. The numbers of words recalled correctly are as follows:

Relaxation		Exercise	
Nonthreat	Threat	Nonthreat	Threat
3	4	2	5
2	4	4	3
3	3	3	4
3	2	3	3
4	4	3	6
3	3	4	5

Perform a two-factor repeated-measures ANOVA and provide a full interpretation of the results.

OVERVIEW AND
FINAL THOUGHTS

SOME TIPS FOR TESTS ON ANALYSIS OF VARIANCE

In class tests, you may be given a set of results, along with a description of the experiment, and asked to analyze the results using an ANOVA. This requires deciding which ANOVA is appropriate and then performing the necessary calculations. This chapter provides a simple strategy for such tests.

Identifying the Design Used to Conduct the Experiment

We know that design and analysis are inseparable. Identifying the design used to run the experiment that provided the results to be analyzed, therefore, will tell us which ANOVA to use. Because we've only considered five designs in detail in this book we'll stick to them for

149

present purposes. This way of thinking, however, can be extended to cover any kind of ANOVA.

To identify which design was used, we need to answer three questions:

1. How many scores did subjects provide? There are two possible answers here:
   a. One
   b. More than one

The answer to this question provides the answer to a different form of the question, namely: Were repeated measures used in the design? If the answer is (a), then no repeated measures were used. If the answer is (b), then at least one factor contains repeated measures.

2. How many distinct influences on the results were there? That is, how many factors are there?

The results represent some kind of scores obtained under at least two conditions (levels). Identify these levels (e.g., light and sound; 10 min, 20 min, and 30 min after drug administration) and you have identified one factor (Type of Stimulus; Time of Test of Performance).

3. Can the subjects in the experiment be split up into two or more identifiable groups?

Thinking about our five designs, the answers to these three questions will identify the design employed to run the experiment. Figure 8.1 represents this approach in the form of a decision tree. Once we have identified which design was used, we just need to answer several other questions (How many subjects are there? How many scores per subject are there? How many levels of each factor are there?) and we can proceed to perform the required analysis.

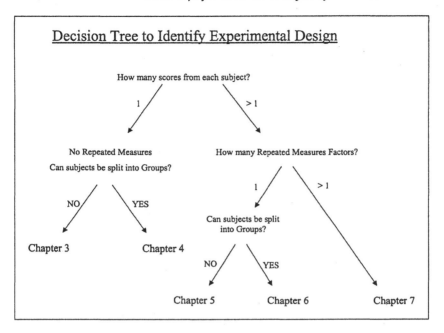

Figure 8.1. Decision tree to identify experimental designs.

Bubble Diagrams

In four chapters (Chapters 3–6), we used bubble diagrams to help us remember the nature of the four designs. Memorizing the four main bubble diagrams (and the associated subsidiary breakdowns in the case of Chapters 4 and 6) is a great way to guide you through these four designs. In the case of the two-factor repeated-measures design (Chapter 7), memorizing the formulas given in Table 7.3 is the best approach.

When using the bubble diagrams, remember that each bubble represents a particular partition of the overall variance, and you need to know which is which. The way we have considered ANOVA will help you to remember these. A useful question here is: Is the variance in this bubble within-subjects or between-subjects variance? Practice drawing the bubble diagrams, then practice filling in the partitioned variance that belongs in each one, and then practice drawing the respective ANOVA summary tables.

Computational Aids for the Necessary Calculations

Once you have identified the design used to generate the results given on your test, you need to perform the actual numerical calculations. Although each of the five designs differs from the others, they all involve the same kinds of calculations. Basically, we take a set of scores, split the set into subgroups in various different ways, and do some addition, some "squaring," and some division.

An extremely helpful way of looking at this process is to remember that *in every calculation we use every score*. One way or another, at some point in all the ANOVAs every score goes into the various subtotals, which are then squared. *These values are then always divided by the number of scores that went into that subtotal.*

For this example, imagine 24 scores. Let's use letters this time. We have not used the letter "X" to avoid possible confusion with the notation symbol "X" representing the scores in a particular group.

A	G	M	S
B	H	N	T
C	I	O	U
D	J	P	V
E	K	Q	Y
F	L	R	Z

No matter what kind of design these scores came from, and therefore what kind of ANOVA we are carrying out on them, this idea of splitting them into subgroups and thus getting subtotals still applies.

Calculation of the Correction Factor

This is $(\sum X)^2/n$. In this example, it is $(A + B + C + \cdots + Z)^2/24$. What we are actually doing here is taking all the scores and making just one subgroup, which actually, therefore, is identical to the group itself. We get our subtotal and divide it by the number of scores that made up that subtotal, that is, 24. Calculation of the correction factor involves one group of 24 subjects.

Calculation of the Total Sum of Squares

This is $\sum X^2 - (\sum X)^2/n$. Here, it is $A^2 + B^2 + C^2 + \cdots + Z^2 - CF$. What we are actually doing here is forming 24 subgroups, each containing just one score. So, when we divide after the squaring process, we divide by the number of scores that made up each total. That is, we divide by 1. Because this division has no mathematical effect (any number divided by 1 is itself), the 1s are never actually shown. If we did show them, the expression would look like this:

$$\frac{A^2}{1} + \frac{B^2}{1} + \frac{C^2}{1} + \cdots + \frac{Z^2}{1} - CF.$$

We therefore have 24 subtotals, each divided by the number of scores that went into that subtotal, that is, 1.

Calculation of Other Sum of Squares Terms

The principle that is evident in the two previous cases (which are the two extremes, because we have one subtotal containing all 24 scores, and 24 subtotals containing one score each) applies to any other calculation. Depending on the analysis in question, we form several specific subgroups. For example:

▶ If we form six subgroups, we will have six subtotals, each squared subtotal being divided by the number of scores making up that subtotal, in this case 4. Note that $6 \times 4 = 24 =$ the overall number of scores.

► If we form four groups, we will have four subtotals, each squared subtotal being divided by 6. Note that $4 \times 6 = 24 =$ overall number of scores.

► If we form two subgroups, we will have two subtotals, each squared subtotal being divided by 12. Note that $2 \times 12 = 24 =$ overall number of scores.

► If we form three subgroups, we will have three subtotals, each squared subtotal being divided by 8. Note that $3 \times 8 = 24$ overall number of scores.

This logic applies to any number of groups that are formed. Therefore, when calculating the SS terms obtained by direct computation from the scores (as opposed to those SS terms found by simple subtraction), this general principle will help you in forming the subgroups and dividing each squared subtotal by the appropriate number.

Interpreting Your Results

When you have completed analyzing the results given on your test and you have your *F* values, you must interpret them in the context of the experiment. We have emphasized throughout the text that the numerical answers provided by the ANOVAs you perform *are not sufficient by themselves; the appropriate interpretations must accompany them.*

The worked examples provided in Chapters 3 through 7 showed you how to interpret the mathematical answers obtained from the analyses conducted. In each case, these mathematical answers were interpreted in the specific context of the experimental results being analyzed. In addition to the *F* value(s) obtained and the level(s) of statistical significance attained, the group means were necessary for this interpretation, particularly in the case of significant findings.

Remember to give a full interpretation of the results of your analyses.

Multiple Comparisons

In some cases, multiple comparisons following an ANOVA are appropriate. We examined the independent-groups *t* test and the dependent-measures *t* test in Chapters 3 and 5, respectively. If you are given questions on tests that require multiple comparisons to be conducted, some instructors may let you know this in the question itself; the question may say "Perform the appropriate ANOVA and subsequent multiple comparisons on the results of the following experiment." Other instructors may leave you to figure this out for yourself.

A simple way to start here is to remember that if a particular factor has only two levels, the *F* value and the two means will provide all the information you need to make a full interpretation of that factor's influence on the results. That is, planned comparisons are only necessary when a factor has more than two levels.

Next, decide which of the two types of *t* tests we discussed is appropriate. For data obtained in an independent-groups design, the independent-groups *t* test is appropriate. For data obtained in a repeated-measures design, the dependent-measures *t* test is appropriate.

To perform either *t* test, you will need to use the appropriate formula. Some instructors may provide these during your class tests. That is, they may put them on the blackboard or on the question sheets. If so, you will not have to memorize the formulas themselves, but you will have to remember which one is appropriate in which context. Other instructors may expect you to remember the formulas themselves. It is perfectly reasonable to ask your instructor about this while preparing for your class tests.

SUMMARY

In this chapter, we have presented some ways of helping you remember various points involved in the calculation of ANOVAs, as well as the calculation of subsequent multiple comparisons. While simply memorizing these strategies may prove useful, it will be of greater benefit to you *if you also understand the logic behind them*. Memory is enhanced by understanding, which provides a conceptual framework onto which to hang individual pieces of information.

An understanding will also help you in the most important part of the analysis—the interpretation of the numbers obtained at the end of the analysis. It is your informed judgment that is the most important part of any statistical analysis.

EVERYDAY BENEFITS OF A FEEL FOR STATISTICS AND FOR EVALUATING DATA

S ome of you may like to take additional classes in statistics and methodology, and to conduct your own experimental behavioral science research. In this case, we hope that we have demonstrated how useful the techniques of ANOVA can be. On the other hand, some of you may have read this book as part of a required course, and, once you have the appropriate course credit, you may not want to think about ANOVAs ever again! Whichever group you fall into, in this final chapter we'd like to show you that a feel for basic statistical concepts and the ability to evaluate claims made by others is very useful in everyday life.

The World of Misleading Data

We are constantly exposed via the print and broadcast media to statements that one candidate's record is better than another's; that

Car A performs far better than Car B; and that, if we purchase a self-improvement course ("Call this 1-800 number in the next ten minutes and your credit card will be billed just three easy payments of $99.99"), we'll almost instantaneously become smarter, thinner, more lovable, a more effective speaker/communicator/negotiator, or anything else our hearts could ever desire. The old quote about three kinds of lies, "lies, damn lies, and statistics," suggests that virtually any picture can be painted with the carefully manipulated use of a few numbers. More realistically, the intentionally misleading use of data can certainly paint the wrong picture, *but only for those who do not know how to evaluate the claims being made.*

Before considering the two main examples in this chapter, consider this anecdotal example. Each time you go shopping in the mall, there seem to be many signs in store windows advertising sales. A common type of sign is one that says "Up to 50% Off." Often, the words "Up to" are in much smaller print than "50% Off," so your first impression is that everything in the store is half-price. On one occasion, one of the authors (JRT) saw a sign in a sports store saying "Up to 70% Off." He went into the store, and was approached by a salesperson. When the salesperson asked if he could help, the author replied that he would like to be shown the items that had been reduced in price by 70%. The salesperson looked completely confused. The author explained that the sign in the window implied that certain items were "70% Off." To cut a long story short, none of the salespersons could find a single item in the store that had been reduced by 70%.

Suppose that the maximum reduction in the store is actually 50%. Does a reduction of 50% allow a window sign legitimately to read "Up to 70% Off"? Both authors would argue that it does not. You can discuss this point with your classmates (and philosophy professors) and see what you all think.

More Substantive Examples

We've emphasized throughout this book that the appropriate interpretation of the results from all of our analyses is crucial in determining what picture the data paint. We'll now use some hypothetical (but nonetheless realistic and relevant) examples to show you that the same type of analytical evaluation of information encountered in everyday life can be very beneficial.

Example 1: Buying a New Car

Consider the graph presented in Figure 9.1, used in promotional literature by the RST Car Company to illustrate how sales of its Model XYZ car are increasing. What information does this graph convey? Actually, we should change the question to a more accurate question: What *impression* is this graph *intended to convey*? Looking at the two columns (or **bars**; this kind of graph is called a **bar graph**), the bar representing "this year" is a lot higher (twice as high) as the column representing "last year." It therefore seems reasonable to assume that twice as many cars were sold this year compared with last year. That is, sales increased 100% year over year.

Taking this argument one step further, what does this suggest to us? Perhaps it suggests that this car is becoming really popular because

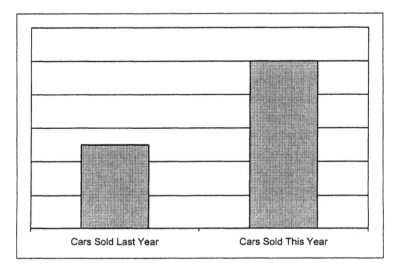

Figure 9.1.

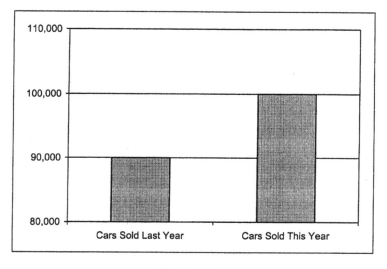

Figure 9.2.

it's a superb car, and that if we want to look cool driving down the highway, the interstate, and our local main street we simply *must* buy one. It is our guess that the RST Car Company would be very happy if you felt this way!

Before you rush out and buy this car, let's use our knowledge of graphs (we discussed this topic in Chapter 4) to examine the actual information "conveyed" by Figure 9.1. First, consider the relative heights of the two bars. As we noted previously, the bar representing sales "this year" is twice as high, as measured from the horizontal axis to the top of the bar, as the bar representing sales "last year." However, *because the vertical axis is not labeled, Figure 9.1 provides no hard data concerning the actual number of sales in either year.*

Imagine that an "Advertising Oversight Committee" told the RST Car Company to provide these hard data in its promotional literature by labeling the vertical axis. Figure 9.2 shows what such a presentation might look like. It now becomes apparent that 90,000 cars were sold "last year" and 100,000 were sold "this year." That is, sales increased 11% year over year, not the 100% increase suggested by Figure 9.1.

Figure 9.2 is therefore a considerable improvement on Figure 9.1, but is still not the most honest presentation of the data. Although the actual

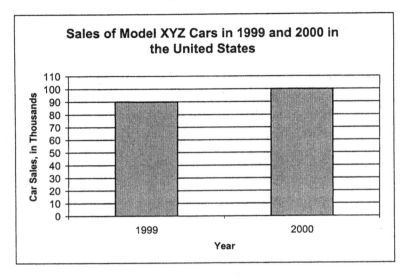

Figure 9.3.

sales numbers are indeed presented on the vertical axis, the axis is not scaled from 0 to 100,000. The bars themselves therefore still convey an image of much greater sales "this year" than "last year." Figure 9.3 corrects this problem.

Figure 9.3 is also much improved over both Figure 9.1 and Figure 9.2 in several other ways. Consider the information on their horizontal axes, that is, "last year" and "this year." More precision would be desirable. Were the two years cited the last two complete calendar years, or the last two 12-month periods? Or, possibly, "last year" may mean "all of the previous calendar year" while "this year" means "the period from January 1 of the current year until last week." We were simply not sure until we saw Figure 9.3.

We also didn't know from Figures 9.1 and 9.2 where these car sales took place. Were they sales in California, Florida, New York, or all of the United States? It was even possible that the sales areas were not comparable from year to year. Suppose that the car was only available in the United States in the first year but was available in Canada, Europe, and Mexico as well in the second year. This means that, while 11% more cars were sold overall in the second year, this increase may be particularly small given that the car was available for sale in many more regional markets in the second year. Also, in this scenario it was possible that *less* cars were sold in the United States in the second year, with the balance being sold abroad. This makes Figures 9.1 and 9.2 even more misleading to potential buyers in the U.S. markets who think that sales are increasing in that country, not decreasing. The full labeling of axes in Figure 9.3, along with the explanatory title provided, gives the reader accurate and readily assimilated data with which to make an informed decision about year-to-year sales of the Model XYZ car.

Example 2: Weight Loss/Dieting Program Advertisements

Consider next the case of advertisements for weight loss programs. At the time of writing this text, approximately 60% of the adult population of the United States is estimated to be either overweight or obese. The conditions are strongly associated with serious diseases such as cardiovascular disease and diabetes. Weight loss/dieting programs, therefore, constitute major businesses.

Advertisements for such programs often include "before" and "after" pictures of an individual who participated in the program and achieved a dramatic weight loss. A statement such as "Thanks to his participation in the Most Amazing Diet Program Ever, Mr. Jones lost 75 lbs. in just 3 months" may accompany the pictures. The question of interest to us is: How well does this information represent the likelihood of our losing the weight we would like to lose if we chose to participate in this program?

First, it should be acknowledged that such advertisements do indeed include a statement somewhere in their presentation that addresses this issue. Very often, this statement is something like "Mr. Jones' results are not typical" or "Individual results may vary." It is also fair to say, however, that these statements are often printed in relatively small print, and that the overall impression that this is an amazing weight loss program can easily be formed after looking at the advertisement.

Back, then, to our question: How well does this information represent the likelihood of our losing the weight we would like to lose if we chose to participate in this program? The answer is simple: very poorly. If 100 people took part in this program, in all likelihood we would get many different results (i.e., many different scores, where each score is "number of pounds lost in a certain length of time"). Two of these results would define the range of weights lost, and it is likely that the 75 lbs. lost by Mr. Jones is the upper limit of the range. As we know, the range is a relatively poor descriptor of a set of scores. What information, then, would provide potential participants in the program with a better way to evaluate its possible benefit to them?

Some representation of the typical weight loss would be helpful, since the advertisement in effect defined Mr. Jones' result as atypical. One of the measures of central tendency described in Chapter 2 (the mode, median, or arithmetic average) would certainly provide more information than simply presenting one atypical result. Providing a measure of central tendency *and* dispersion around that central value would be even better.

While this type of information would be helpful, though, it still doesn't give potential clients all the information that may be helpful in deciding whether to sign up for the program. For example, exercise may be a central component of a particular weight loss program. Moderate exercise (under the supervision of a physician where appropriate) can be a very effective component of an overall weight loss program, and for potential clients who are not already exercising this program may therefore be a good choice. For other potential clients who are already taking regular exercise, however, the benefit of this component of the program, and therefore possibly the program as a whole, may be considerably less.

Similar logic may well apply to several components of any program. Certain potential clients will benefit more from specific components of the program than others, which, in turn, means that individuals fitting Profile A are much more likely to benefit from certain programs than individuals fitting Profile B, and visa versa. It is therefore a good idea to do as much research on a program of interest before signing up.

SUMMARY

The general point to be made from these two examples (and you can probably think of many related examples) is that a single piece of information, even if absolutely accurate, can be misleading. A more thorough investigation and *appropriate evaluation* of all available data provide a much more solid basis for making an informed decision. Information is power, and the ability to evaluate information appropriately is extremely powerful. Throughout the examples of statistical analyses presented in this book we have emphasized the importance of the correct (appropriate) interpretation of the mathematical answers obtained. The same strategy of data evaluation can serve you extremely well in all sorts of everyday situations.

APPENDIX

A

Tables of Critical Values of F^*

TABLE A1.   5% Critical Values ($p = 0.05$)

	Degrees of Freedom for the Numerator									
	1	2	3	4	5	6	8	12	24	∞
1	161.4	199.5	215.7	224.6	230.2	234.0	238.9	243.9	249.0	254.3
2	18.51	19.00	19.16	19.25	19.30	19.33	19.37	19.41	19.45	19.50
3	10.13	9.55	9.28	9.12	9.01	8.94	8.84	8.74	8.64	8.53
4	7.71	6.94	6.59	6.39	6.26	6.16	6.04	5.91	5.77	5.63
5	6.61	5.79	5.41	5.19	5.05	4.95	4.82	4.68	4.53	4.36
6	5.99	5.14	4.76	4.53	4.39	4.28	4.15	4.00	3.84	3.67
7	5.59	4.74	4.35	4.12	3.97	3.87	3.73	3.57	3.41	3.23
8	5.32	4.46	4.07	3.84	3.69	3.58	3.44	3.28	3.12	2.93
9	5.12	4.26	3.86	3.63	3.48	3.37	3.23	3.07	2.90	2.71
10	4.96	4.10	3.71	3.48	3.33	3.22	3.07	2.91	2.74	2.54
11	4.84	3.98	3.59	3.36	3.20	3.09	2.95	2.79	2.61	2.40
12	4.75	3.88	3.49	3.26	3.11	3.00	2.85	2.69	2.50	2.30
13	4.67	3.80	3.41	3.18	3.02	2.92	2.77	2.60	2.42	2.21
14	4.60	3.74	3.34	3.11	2.96	2.85	2.70	2.53	2.35	2.13
15	4.54	3.68	3.29	3.06	2.90	2.79	2.64	2.48	2.29	2.07
16	4.49	3.63	3.24	3.01	2.85	2.74	2.59	2.42	2.24	2.01
17	4.45	3.59	3.20	2.96	2.81	2.70	2.55	2.38	2.19	1.96
18	4.41	3.55	3.16	2.93	2.77	2.66	2.51	2.34	2.15	1.92
19	4.38	3.52	3.13	2.90	2.74	2.63	2.48	2.31	2.11	1.88
20	4.35	3.49	3.10	2.87	2.71	2.60	2.45	2.28	2.08	1.84
21	4.32	3.47	3.07	2.84	2.68	2.57	2.42	2.25	2.05	1.81
22	4.30	3.44	3.05	2.82	2.66	2.55	2.40	2.23	2.03	1.78
23	4.28	3.42	3.03	2.80	2.64	2.53	2.38	2.20	2.00	1.76
24	4.26	3.40	3.01	2.78	2.62	2.51	2.36	2.18	1.98	1.73
25	4.24	3.38	2.99	2.76	2.60	2.49	2.34	2.16	1.96	1.71
26	4.22	3.37	2.98	2.74	2.59	2.47	2.32	2.15	1.95	1.69
27	4.21	3.35	2.96	2.73	2.57	2.46	2.30	2.13	1.93	1.67
28	4.20	3.34	2.95	2.71	2.56	2.44	2.29	2.12	1.91	1.65
29	4.18	3.33	2.93	2.70	2.54	2.43	2.28	2.10	1.90	1.64
30	4.17	3.32	2.92	2.69	2.53	2.42	2.27	2.09	1.89	1.62
40	4.08	3.23	2.84	2.61	2.45	2.34	2.18	2.00	1.79	1.51
60	4.00	3.15	2.76	2.52	2.37	2.25	2.10	1.92	1.70	1.39
120	3.92	3.07	2.68	2.45	2.29	2.17	2.02	1.83	1.61	1.25
∞	3.84	2.99	2.60	2.37	2.21	2.10	1.94	1.75	1.52	1.00

Degrees of Freedom for the Denominator

*Adapted from Table V of R. A. Fisher and F. Yates, "Statistical Tables for Biological, Agricultural and Medical Research," 6th Edition, Oliver and Boyd, Ltd., Edinburgh. (Reprinted, 1974, by the Longman Group, Ltd., London.) Used with permission of Pearson Education, Ltd.

TABLE A2.   1% Critical Values ($p = 0.01$)

		Degrees of Freedom for the Numerator								
	1	2	3	4	5	6	8	12	24	∞
1	4052	4999	5403	5625	5764	5859	5982	6106	6234	6366
2	98.50	99.00	99.17	99.25	99.30	99.33	99.37	99.42	99.46	99.50
3	34.12	30.82	29.46	28.71	28.24	27.91	27.49	27.05	26.60	26.12
4	21.20	18.00	16.69	15.98	15.52	15.21	14.80	14.37	13.93	13.46
5	16.26	13.27	12.06	11.39	10.97	10.67	10.29	9.89	9.47	9.02
6	13.74	10.92	9.78	9.15	8.75	8.47	8.10	7.72	7.31	6.88
7	12.25	9.55	8.45	7.85	7.46	7.19	6.84	6.47	6.07	5.65
8	11.26	8.65	7.59	7.01	6.63	6.37	6.03	5.67	5.28	4.86
9	10.56	8.02	6.99	6.42	6.06	5.80	5.47	5.11	4.73	4.31
10	10.04	7.56	6.55	5.99	5.64	5.39	5.06	4.71	4.33	3.91
11	9.65	7.20	6.22	5.67	5.32	5.07	4.74	4.40	4.02	3.60
12	9.33	6.93	5.95	5.41	5.06	4.82	4.50	4.16	3.78	3.36
13	9.07	6.70	5.74	5.20	4.86	4.62	4.30	3.96	3.59	3.16
14	8.86	6.51	5.56	5.03	4.69	4.46	4.14	3.80	3.43	3.00
15	8.68	6.36	5.42	4.89	4.56	4.32	4.00	3.67	3.29	2.87
16	8.53	6.23	5.29	4.77	4.44	4.20	3.89	3.55	3.18	2.75
17	8.40	6.11	5.18	4.67	4.34	4.10	3.79	3.45	3.08	2.65
18	8.28	6.01	5.09	4.58	4.25	4.01	3.71	3.37	3.00	2.57
19	8.18	5.93	5.01	4.50	4.17	3.94	3.63	3.30	2.92	2.49
20	8.10	5.85	4.94	4.43	4.10	3.87	3.56	3.23	2.86	2.42
21	8.02	5.78	4.87	4.37	4.04	3.81	3.51	3.17	2.80	2.36
22	7.94	5.72	4.82	4.31	3.99	3.76	3.45	3.12	2.75	2.31
23	7.88	5.66	4.76	4.26	3.94	3.71	3.41	3.07	2.70	2.26
24	7.82	5.61	4.72	4.22	3.90	3.67	3.36	3.03	2.66	2.21
25	7.77	5.57	4.68	4.18	3.86	3.63	3.32	2.99	2.62	2.17
26	7.72	5.53	4.64	4.14	3.82	3.59	3.29	2.96	2.58	2.13
27	7.68	5.49	4.60	4.11	3.78	3.56	3.26	2.93	2.55	2.10
28	7.64	5.45	4.57	4.07	3.75	3.53	3.23	2.90	2.52	2.06
29	7.60	5.42	4.54	4.04	3.73	3.50	3.20	2.87	2.49	2.03
30	7.56	5.39	4.51	4.02	3.70	3.47	3.17	2.84	2.47	2.01
40	7.31	5.18	4.31	3.83	3.51	3.29	2.99	2.66	2.29	1.80
60	7.08	4.98	4.13	3.65	3.34	3.12	2.82	2.50	2.12	1.60
120	6.85	4.79	3.95	3.48	3.17	2.96	2.66	2.34	1.95	1.38
∞	6.64	4.60	3.78	3.32	3.02	2.80	2.51	2.18	1.79	1.00

Degrees of Freedom for the Denominator

APPENDIX

B

t-TABLE

Table of Critical Values of t; 5% and 1% Values[*]

df	p	
	0.05	0.01
1	12.706	63.657
2	4.303	9.925
3	3.182	5.841
4	2.776	4.604
5	2.571	4.032
6	2.447	3.707
7	2.365	3.499
8	2.306	3.355
9	2.262	3.250
10	2.228	3.169
11	2.201	3.106
12	2.179	3.055
13	2.160	3.012
14	2.145	2.977
15	2.131	2.947
16	2.120	2.921
17	2.110	2.898
18	2.101	2.878
19	2.093	2.861
20	2.086	2.845
21	2.080	2.831
22	2.074	2.819
23	2.069	2.807
24	2.064	2.797
25	2.060	2.787
26	2.056	2.779
27	2.052	2.771
28	2.048	2.763
29	2.045	2.756
30	2.042	2.750
40	2.021	2.704
60	2.000	2.660
120	1.980	2.617
∞	1.960	2.576

[*]Adapted from Table III of R. A. Fisher and F. Yates, "Statistical Tables for Biological, Agricultural and Medical Research," 6th Edition, Oliver and Boyd, Ltd., Edinburgh. (Reprinted, 1974, by the Longman Group, Ltd., London.) Used with permission of Pearson Education, Ltd.

ANSWERS

This appendix provides the answers to the two exercises that are given in Chapters 3 through 7.

▬ Chapter 3

3.1

Interpretation: The two factories did not differ significantly in the average number of sick days.

3.2

$$F(1,8) = 3.27, \qquad p = \text{ns}.$$

Interpretation: Groups A and B did not differ significantly on their estimation of time.

▬ Chapter 4

4.1

Interpretation:
Persons that did aerobic exercise had significantly lower heart rates than those that did not do aerobic exercise.
Persons that did strength training did not have significantly different heart rates compared to those that did not do strength training.
The effect of aerobic training did not differentially effect those that did strength training compared to those that did not do strength training.

4.2

Main effect of gender:
$$F(1,12) = 4.74, \qquad p = \text{ns},$$
Main effect of examination method:
$$F(1,12) = 1.57, \qquad p = \text{ns},$$
Interaction of gender and exam method:
$$F(1,12) = 25.82, \qquad p < 0.01.$$

Interpretation: Males and females did not differ significantly. Examination methods did not differ significant across all subjects. However, there is a highly significant interaction such that males scored better on the multiple choice exam and females scored better on the essay exam.

▬ *Chapter 5*

5.1

Interpretation: Pilots reacted significantly more slowly after 30 hours of sleep deprivation.

5.2

$$F(1,5) = 40.00, \qquad p < 0.01.$$

Interpretation: Athletes committed significantly less errors after training.

▬ *Chapter 6*

6.1

Interpretation:
The depressed and the nondepressed groups did not differ significantly on negative mood scores. The negative mood scores for the happy and sad memories did not differ significantly. In addition, the presence or absence of depression did not differentially influence the scores on the negative mood measure for the happy and sad memories.

6.2

Main effect of education level (high school vs college):
$$F(1,8) = 130.0, \qquad p < 0.01,$$
Main effect of time:
$$F(1,8) = 54.5, \qquad p < 0.01,$$
Interaction of education level and time:
$$F(1,8) = 1.46, \qquad p = \text{ns}.$$

Interpretation: College students committed significantly less errors than high school students, and both groups performed better at Time 2 compared to Time 1. However, education level did not differentially affect errors committed at Time 1 compared to Time 2.

▬ Chapter 7

7.1

Interpretation: Muscle strength was significantly less in space than on Earth. The strength scores were not different on the first test compared to the second test and being on Earth or in space did not differentially affect the strength scores for the two repetitions.

7.2

Main effect of condition (relaxation vs exercise):
$F(1,5) = 8.45,$ $p < 0.05,$
Main effect of word type (non-threat vs threat):
$F(1,5) = 4.35,$ $p = \text{ns},$
Interaction of condition and word type:
$F(1,5) = 1.00,$ $p = \text{ns}.$

Interpretation: Anxious patients recalled significantly more words after exercise. Anxious patients did not differ in their recall of non-threat and threat words. In addition, anxious patients did not differentially recall non-threat or threat words when they were relaxed compared to when they had exercised.

INDEX

ABOUT THE AUTHORS

Rick Turner is an experimental psychologist who has spent 15 years conducting research in the field of cardiovascular behavioral medicine, investigating the effects of stress on the cardiovascular system and the possible role of stress-induced responses in the development of cardiovascular disease. He has published over 50 research papers and book chapters describing his collaborative cardiovascular research, and three books on the role of behavior in health and disease. His text *Cardiovascular Reactivity and Stress: Patterns of Cardiovascular Response* (New York: Plenum Press, 1994) introduced the methodology and findings of cardiovascular reactivity research to undergraduate and graduate students.

Dr. Turner has received research awards from the Society for Psychophysiological Research and the American Psychosomatic Society, and he is a Fellow of the Society of Behavioral Medicine. He lives in Chapel Hill, North Carolina, where he provides scientific consulting, writing, and editing services for biomedical research projects and for the pharmaceutical and biotechnology industries. He enjoys sports, travel, and Italian restaurants.

Julian Thayer received his Ph.D. from New York University in psychophysiology with a minor in quantitative methods. He has published over 60 research papers and book chapters covering a wide range of topics, including research design and multivariate statistical techniques. Over the past 16 years, he has taught courses on research design and statistical analysis to students and faculty throughout the United States and Europe.

Dr. Thayer has received research awards from Sigma Xi and the American Psychosomatic Society, and he is a member of the Academy of Behavioral Medicine Research. He has also received a Fulbright Fellowship to conduct research in Norway. He lives in Baltimore, where he is currently employed as a Special Expert by the National Institute on Aging. In addition, he is a professional jazz musician with several recordings to his credit.

CPSIA information can be obtained
at www.ICGtesting.com
Printed in the USA
FFHW021112221219
57141322-62710FF